JESUS

JESUS

WHY THE WORLD IS STILL

FASCINATED BY HIM

TIM LAHAYE

WITH DAVID MINASIAN

David C Cook

transforming lives together

JESUS
Published by David C. Cook
4050 Lee Vance View
Colorado Springs, CO 80918 U.S.A.

David C. Cook Distribution Canada
55 Woodslee Avenue, Paris, Ontario, Canada N3L 3E5

David C. Cook U.K., Kingsway Communications
Eastbourne, East Sussex BN23 6NT, England

The Web site addresses recommended throughout this book are offered as a
resource to you. These Web sites are not intended in any way to be or imply an
endorsement on the part of David C. Cook, nor do we vouch for their content.

Scripture taken from the New King James Version. Copyright © 1982
by Thomas Nelson, Inc. Used by permission. All rights reserved.
Italics in Scripture are added by the authors for emphasis.

LCCN 2009927673
Hardcover ISBN 978-1-4347-6625-0
ITPE ISBN 978-1-4347-6535-2
eISBN 978-1-4347-0038-4

© 2009 Tim LaHaye
Published in association with the literary agencies of WordServe Literary
Group, Ltd., 10152 S. Knoll Circle, Highlands Ranch, CO 80130
(www.wordserveliterary.com), and Intellectual Property Group of Los Angeles, California.

The Team: Don Pape, Brian Thomasson, Amy Kiechlin,
Sarah Schultz, Jaci Schneider, and Karen Athen
Cover Design: James Hall, JWH Graphic Arts
Cover Photos: iStockphoto, royalty-free

Hardcover printed in Canada
First Edition 2009

1 2 3 4 5 6 7 8 9 10

051209

To all honest seekers of truth who are searching for commonsense reasons to believe in Jesus Christ.

To all who already believe Jesus is the Son of God.

And to all who wonder why, after two thousand years, the world is still fascinated by Him.

Contents

Chapter One

WHY JESUS?

To invoke a well-worn cliché, truth is indeed stranger than fiction. Never in a million years would a novelist or playwright attempt to create such a story ... a story of a young carpenter from an obscure village who would go on to become the most influential person in all of history ... a story of a man who would continue to impact the world two thousand years after His execution ... a story of a man who could miraculously heal the sick, predict the future, and even rise from the dead! No one would ever believe such a story ... right?

Well ...

It has been estimated that there are currently between seventy and one hundred million people in America alone who do indeed believe such a story, and as many as two billion more worldwide.[1] Not only are most of these people convinced the story is true, they have gone so far as to stake their eternal destinies upon it.

Influence Far and Wide

During a break from our TV interview on *Larry King Live* in March of 2006, Larry surprised Jerry Jenkins and me with this statement: "I am not a believer, but I have the utmost respect for Jesus Christ. I believe He was the most influential person who ever lived."

Why would Larry King make such a statement?

Because it's true.

Of the estimated more than thirteen billion people who have lived on the earth since the dawn of recorded history, why does the one named Jesus Christ draw so much attention—more attention without question than any other person? The world has always been, is now, and will forever be fascinated by Jesus. But why?

Before we attempt to answer that question, let's consider the facts: He has served as the inspiration for more literature, more music, and more works of art than any other person in history. Millions of churches throughout the world have been built in His honor. Our calendar has been set according to His birth. The two biggest holidays celebrated worldwide each year, Christmas and Easter, commemorate His birth and His resurrection. Nearly everyone who has lived on this planet during the last two millennia has heard of Him. Is there any other person who comes to mind for which the same can be said?

Amazingly, His influence in the world has not diminished over the course of the succeeding centuries. Despite ever-evolving cultural changes and notwithstanding media reports to the contrary, Jesus is just as relevant to this generation as He was when He walked the shores of Galilee. Throughout the ages, people inspired by His teachings have taken the initiative to build the majority of the world's hospitals, instigate the formation of most of our colleges and universities, and launch countless humanitarian programs in nearly every part of the globe.

Even those who discount the miraculous side of Jesus' persona nevertheless find His teachings to be astute and infused with wisdom. Secularists and followers of other religions alike seem compelled, at the very least, to esteem Him as a great teacher or wise sage. However, simply having an abundant level of intellectual insight doesn't really begin to account for the amount of adoration Jesus has received during the past two thousand years. Have there been other great thinkers and philosophers down through the ages who are as worthy? Confucius, Descartes, Hume, Kant, Kierkegaard, Marx, Nietzsche, Rousseau, Russell, and Sartre are names familiar to those who have studied the subject of philosophy. Has the level of devotion to any of these men risen to even a fraction of that which has been afforded Jesus?

Then there are the "big three" of the ancient Greek philosophers—Socrates, Plato, and Aristotle—who together are said to have formed the philosophical foundation of Western culture.[2] And yet, despite being in the public eye for *only three and a half years*, Jesus and His teachings have arguably impacted the world far more than the collective erudition of these three great philosophers whose combined careers totaled *more than 150 years*.

Still, there are others who deem the attributes of Jesus to extend far beyond that of mere wisdom. Many believe Jesus to be a prophet, a Messiah, even God in human form. And it is these claims that have motivated some to go to great lengths to try to curtail His influence in the world. Down through the centuries untold millions of Christian martyrs have been subjected to horribly agonizing deaths on account of their allegiance to Jesus, beginning with the stoning of the apostle Stephen shortly after the crucifixion of Christ[3] and continuing ever since. By the Middle Ages, the various types of torture and killing devices used on Christians had become so grisly as to almost defy description. It seems there was no shortage of creative ways in which martyrs could be stretched, burned, flayed, sawed, pierced, hung, boiled, or drowned.

The Writing on the Wall

Throughout history countless writers have felt compelled to publish their personal perspectives on the historical facts surrounding Jesus and His teachings. The works of second-century writers such as Irenaeus and Tertullian, for example, support those of the New Testament writers Matthew, Mark, Luke, and John. Other apologists (defenders of the faith) from Augustine to Francis Schaeffer followed in succeeding centuries.

Of course, there have been numerous detractors as well throughout the last two millennia. One such author was Englishman H. G. Wells. Although overshadowed by his famous science fiction works that included *The War of the Worlds, The Time Machine,* and *The Invisible Man*, Wells was also a prolific writer of nonfiction. One of his efforts, titled *The Outline of History*, was a twelve-hundred-page volume that traced the history of our planet from its supposed primordial origins up through World War I.

Wells was an outspoken socialist and ardent promoter of Darwin's theory of evolution. And he was certainly no fan of Jesus of Nazareth. It therefore must have come as a bit of a shock to discover that upon the completion of his manuscript, Wells had devoted a staggering forty-one pages to Jesus Christ, which turned out to be a far larger amount than he had bestowed on any other historical person mentioned in the work, including his personal hero, Plato, who received a mere two-page mention from the writer.[4]

Likewise, the secular *Encyclopaedia Britannica* in a recent edition saw
fit to dedicate more than 21,000 words to Jesus Christ, which turned out
to be the largest of any of its biographical entries, surpassing that of former
President Bill Clinton, who collected only 2,511 words.[5]

A more compassionate oeuvre of Jesus can be found written by the
celebrated nineteenth-century American author Mark Twain. In his
1869 publication *The Innocents Abroad*, Twain recounted his travels
through the Holy Land, and in particular the city where Jesus spent
His youth:

> In the starlight, Galilee has no boundaries but the
> broad compass of the heavens, and is a theater meet for
> great events; meet for the birth of a religion able to save
> the world; and meet for the stately Figure appointed to
> stand upon its stage and proclaim its high decrees.[6]

Although not as well known as some of his other works such as *The
Adventures of Huckleberry Finn*, *The Innocents Abroad* became Twain's
biggest-selling book during his lifetime.[7]

In more recent times there has been the unprecedented (and unex-
pected) success of the Left Behind series of novels written by myself and my
cowriter Jerry Jenkins. This fictionalized account of the *last days* scenario as
presented in the book of Revelation has struck a chord with readers who
have been looking forward with anticipation to the promised return of the
Lord Jesus Christ. With sixteen books in the series and more than seventy
million copies sold, it has become one of the biggest-selling adult fiction
series of all time, no doubt due to our readers' fascination with Jesus and
the subject of biblical prophecy.

Extra, Extra—Read All about It

If you were to look closely at America's three leading newsmagazines—*Time, Newsweek,* and *U.S. News & World Report*—you might notice a rather odd recurring phenomenon. These magazines are dedicated to covering the top political, economic, scientific, and entertainment news from around the world each week. And although they occasionally touch on religious issues, these would certainly not be classified as religious publications. And yet, they have placed Jesus Christ on their covers more than two dozen times in the last decade! In fact, Jesus has appeared on more covers of *Time* than any other person who has ever lived, with the exception of the last few U.S. presidents.[8] It begs the question as to why these news organizations *who deal primarily with current events* would find the details surrounding a Jewish carpenter from an insignificant Middle Eastern village who lived and died two thousand years ago so compelling as to feature cover stories about Him again and again. What's going on?

    Time magazine itself has featured Jesus on its cover an astonishing twenty-one times during the last seven decades—and that's in addition to another sixty-five cover stories dealing with the subject of Christianity during this same period.[9] To put this in perspective, examine the following list, which chronicles the number of times each of these other famous individuals (excluding recent U.S. presidents) have appeared on the cover of *Time* since the beginning of World War II:

    Jesus Christ—21
    Mikhail Gorbachev—14
    Saddam Hussein—14
    Henry Kissinger—11
    Nelson Rockefeller—11
    Al Gore—10

Fidel Castro—8

Princess Diana—8

Bill Gates—8

Joseph Stalin—8

Spiro Agnew—7

Yasser Arafat—7

Douglas MacArthur—6

O. J. Simpson—6

Mao Tse-tung—6

Winston Churchill—5

Thomas Dewey—5

Newt Gingrich—5

John Kerry—5

Martin Luther King—5

Osama bin Laden—5

Yitzhak Rabin—5

The Beatles—4

Dick Cheney—4

Albert Einstein—4

John Glenn—4

Billy Graham—4

Adolph Hitler—4

Howard Hughes—4

Monica Lewinsky—4

Nelson Mandela—4

Colin Powell—4

Darth Vader—4

George Washington—4

Woody Allen—3

Tom Cruise—3

Walt Disney—3

Jesse Jackson—3

Shirley MacLaine—3

Oliver North—3

George Patton—3

Dan Rather—3

Steven Spielberg—3

Marlon Brando—2

Bill Cosby—2

Sigmund Freud—2

Alan Greenspan—2

J. Edgar Hoover—2

Thomas Jefferson—2

Stephen King—2

Rush Limbaugh—2

Marilyn Monroe—2

Ross Perot—2

Harry Potter—2

Frank Sinatra—2

Bruce Springsteen—2

John Travolta—2

Ted Turner—2

John Wayne—2

Benjamin Franklin—1

Abraham Lincoln—1

Mother Teresa—1

Curiously, the news magazines of today that feature a portrait of Jesus on their covers are most often accompanied by stories that give credibility to ancient *Gnostic* ideas while simultaneously undercutting proven historical biblical data. Taken from the Greek word meaning *knowledge*, Gnosticism primarily teaches that the human soul is divine and is trapped in a material world created by an imperfect god. In order to escape this inferior world, one must obtain esoteric spiritual knowledge reserved only for an elite few.

Frequently, these magazine articles claim to clear up some *ancient mystery*, reveal some *hidden secret*, or offer some *new insights*. In nearly every case the readers are asked to jettison their traditional beliefs about Christianity or encouraged to merge their "outdated" views of Christ with more "intellectually sound" Gnostic concepts. Often these *new discoveries* and *new appraisals* are nothing more than variations of old Gnostic ideas, which are based on second- or third-century documents of dubious origins that have been repackaged to appeal to a postmodern culture.

Similarly, there has been a resurgence of these identical Gnostic ideas in a number of recent high-profile books whose primary objective, it appears, is to undermine the historical facts surrounding the life of Jesus. Chief among such modern-day pro-Gnostic tomes is *The Da Vinci Code* by author Dan Brown, which spent more than two years on the *New York Times* best-seller list. Its revisionist claims include the assertions that Jesus was married and that His divinity was a concept invented by the Emperor Constantine in AD 325. When confronted with proof of the innumerable historical errors contained in the book, Brown defenders simply sidestep the issue by stating that *The Da Vinci Code* is a work of fiction.[10]

A plethora of other like-minded books are on the market, such as *The Jesus Papers* by mysticism expert Michael Baigent; *The Jesus Dynasty* by religious studies professor James Tabor; *Beyond Belief* by Gnostic specialist Elaine Pagels; and *Misquoting Jesus* by lapsed evangelical Bart Ehrman, all of which, unlike *The Da Vinci Code*, make no claim of being fictional. These books elaborate on many of Gnosticism's theories, including the idea that Jesus didn't actually die as a result of the crucifixion, that the resurrection was fraudulently staged, and that the Bible is so filled with textual errors as to be completely worthless.

Traditional Christians would claim that today's revival and promotion of Gnosticism amounts to nothing more than a full frontal attack on the basic doctrines of Christianity. Gnostic promoters, on the other hand, would say that biblical doctrines were corrupted from the start and that only now is the full truth being revealed. So who is to be believed?

Hurray for Hollywood

Not surprisingly, the success of the book *The Da Vinci Code* caught the eye of Hollywood producers shortly after it made its way to the top of the best-sellers list. Noted actor Tom Hanks teamed up with film director Ron Howard to bring Brown's thriller to the big screen in 2006. The film ended up grossing more than $200 million domestically and was heralded as a bona fide success by the media.[11] Many of the same anti-Christian themes that had permeated the book made it onto the screen.

Two years earlier, another Jesus-themed motion picture, Mel Gibson's *The Passion of the Christ*, had taken Hollywood by surprise. Gibson's film did better than *The Da Vinci Code* at the domestic box office, bringing in more than $370 million.[12] However, both films would ultimately succeed beyond anyone's expectations by generating in excess of $1 billion each once the foreign box office receipts and DVD sales had been counted.

Theologically speaking, the two films could not have been further apart. For many, *The Passion*, despite its reliance on some nonbiblical texts, was seen as an attempt to make a film that was somewhat faithful to the Scriptures upon which it was based. This was, to say the least, astonishing for a film produced and directed by a major Hollywood insider. *The Da Vinci Code,* on the other hand, was more typical of Hollywood and was seen as a blatant attack against various biblical precepts that millions hold dear. Media watchers were painfully aware of the double standard that had been employed by the studios regarding the production and distribution of these two films. As expected, *The Da Vinci Code* was enthusiastically embraced and promoted through the Hollywood system while *The Passion* was thwarted at every stage of its production and distribution. Only through Mel Gibson's tenacity and resourcefulness (financial and otherwise) was *The Passion* able to eventually see the light of day.

However, what is truly amazing in all this is that here were two major modern-day Hollywood films whose story lines, despite the polarity of their theology, revolved around a Jewish carpenter who hailed from an insignificant little town twenty centuries ago. And yet these films were still culturally relevant, controversial, and able to generate billions of dollars—two thousand years after the fact!

Who Do You Say I Am?

The Bible records an important exchange that took place between Jesus and His disciples while they were visiting various towns in the region of Caesarea Philippi. Jesus had been praying alone when He was suddenly approached by His disciples. As they began to walk together along the road, Jesus turned and asked two crucial questions. So significant was this discussion that it was recorded in the first three books of the New Testament (referred to as the Synoptic Gospels)—in Matthew 16, Mark 8, and Luke 9:

When Jesus came into the region of Caesarea Philippi, He asked His disciples, saying, "Who do men say that I, the Son of Man, am?" So they said, "Some say John the Baptist, some Elijah, and others Jeremiah or one of the prophets." He said to them, "But who do you say that I am?" Simon Peter answered and said, "You are the Christ, the Son of the living God." Jesus answered and said to him, "Blessed are you, Simon Bar-Jonah, for flesh and blood has not revealed this to you, but My Father who is in heaven." (Matthew 16:13–17)

Peter, who was known for his impetuousness when it came to speaking out, may not have fully understood the implication of what he was saying at this point in time. Not only was Peter affirming that Jesus was indeed the Messiah, the literal fulfillment of Old Testament prophecies, but that He was also deity—God in human flesh.

Today, these remain the two most important questions anyone can ask … "Who do men say that I [Jesus] am?" and "Who do *you* say that I am?" Your answers to these questions will determine the course of your life along with your eternal destiny.

Whenever I have been interviewed by various television and radio talk show hosts such as Larry King, Bill O'Reilly, Morley Safer, Glenn Beck, or others, the question invariably comes up: "Why do you say believing in Jesus Christ is the only way to heaven?" The answer is found in who He is. If He is truly "the only begotten Son of God, born of a virgin" as the Bible presents Him, then He qualifies as the only way to salvation, since He said of Himself:

I am the way, the truth, and the life. No one comes to the Father except through Me. (John 14:6)

But if this thirty-three-year-old Galilean carpenter was just another of the estimated thirteen billion people who have lived on the earth, then the devotion of those who esteem (or hate) Him is surely misguided. In any event, we must answer a critical question … *Why after two thousand years is the world still fascinated with Jesus?*

Chapter Two

JESUS AND HIS BEST-SELLING BOOK

Although literally thousands of ancient documents refer to various aspects of the life of Christ, the most complete source of information about Jesus comes from the manuscripts that make up the Bible. Ever since first rolling off Johannes Gutenberg's original printing press in Strasbourg, Germany, in 1455, the Bible has gone on to become the biggest-selling book in all of history:

> No one really knows how many copies of the Bible have been printed, sold, or distributed. The Bible Society's attempt to calculate the number printed between 1816 and 1975 produced the figure of 2,458,000,000. A more recent survey, for the years up to 1992, put it closer to 6,000,000,000 in more than 2,000 languages and dialects. Whatever the precise figure, the Bible is by far the bestselling book of all time.[1]

Over the centuries, the Bible has withstood the test of time and, despite unending controversy, or perhaps in part because of it, continues to annually outsell all other books. The *New York Times* and other such publications that are responsible for compiling best-seller lists decided long ago to forgo the inclusion of the Bible at the number-one position each week, apparently due to redundancy:

> The familiar observation that the Bible is the best-selling book of all time obscures a more startling fact: the Bible is the best-selling book of the year, every year. Calculating how many Bibles are sold in the United States is a virtually impossible task, but a conservative estimate is that in 2005 Americans purchased some twenty-five million Bibles—twice as many as the most recent Harry Potter book.[2]

The Bible: A Brief History

The Bible of today consists of sixty-six different subbooks written by forty different authors over a period of about fifteen hundred years. The Old Testament, which is made up of thirty-nine of these books, predates the time of Christ—although much of the content centers around the prophesied future appearance of the Messiah (see chapter 3). The first five books of the Old Testament, consisting of Genesis, Exodus, Leviticus, Numbers, and Deuteronomy, are collectively known as the Torah or Pentateuch and are believed to have been written by Moses during the mid-fifteenth century BC, while the final Old Testament book, Malachi, dates to the mid -fifth century BC. The Old Testament contains a tremendous amount of information including details about the creation, the flood, the formation of language, the origin of the Jewish people, the establishment of kings, and numerous prophecies.

The New Testament contains twenty-seven books, all of which focus on the person of Jesus Christ. Written over a period of about fifty years during the second half of the first century AD, these books consist of four different versions of the life of Christ (the gospels of Matthew, Mark, Luke, and John); a book that describes what happened to the disciples following the resurrection (the book of Acts); letters of instruction to churches in various cities (such as the books of Corinthians and Ephesians, etc.); and a book of prophecy that details the future events of the *last days* (the book of Revelation).

From start to finish, the Bible presents an epic account of God's relationship with His most precious creation: mankind. So how did this "collection of books within a Book" come together? The writer of the book of Hebrews in the New Testament provides us with a clue:

> God, who at various times and in various ways spoke in
> time past to the fathers by the prophets, has in these last
> days spoken to us by His Son. (Hebrews 1:1–2)

The Old Testament came into being as a result of God "speaking" to His chosen prophets *"in time past"* (prior to the time of Christ). These men, who came from all walks of life, were given the task to write down His divine message for eventual dissemination to the people. Why were prophets chosen rather than religious leaders? Because they could be counted on to not corrupt the information with their own thoughts or ideas (see chapter 3 to discover the penalty that awaited any prophet who spoke on his own accord while claiming to be speaking on God's behalf). *"Various times and in various ways"* is an indication of the separate occasions where God provided His message to His prophets. This resulted in the books of the Old Testament being written at different points over a one-thousand-year time frame, from about 1450 BC to 435 BC. King David, who wrote many of the Bible's psalms, which include prophecies about the coming Messiah, knew that it was the Lord who was instructing him what to write:

> "All this," said David, "the LORD made me understand in writing, by His hand upon me." (1 Chronicles 28:19)

The New Testament, as indicated by the author of Hebrews, came about as a result of the apostles' documentation of the information *"spoken to us by His Son"* Jesus Christ. Some, like Matthew and John, were disciples of Jesus, while the apostle Paul, who was originally an enemy of Christ, was later drafted into the ministry following the resurrection. Luke, the writer of the book of Acts and the gospel that bears his name, was a noted doctor, historian, and researcher. Although not an original disciple, he nevertheless carefully interviewed eyewitnesses to the events of Christ's life while traveling with the apostle Paul on a number of missionary journeys. Together, the Old and New Testaments provide us with the complete written *Word of God*, the result of a unique and supernatural cooperative communication between God and man.

Preserving the Text

> All Scripture is given by inspiration of God, and is profitable for doctrine, for reproof, for correction, for instruction in righteousness. (2 Timothy 3:16)

Most of the books of the Old and New Testaments were originally written in the Hebrew, Aramaic, or Greek language upon *papyrus*, a plant used to create scrolls and pages; or *parchment*, which was made from animal skin. The original manuscripts, written in the author's own handwriting (or the handwriting of his personal scribe), are referred to as the *original autographs*. It is these manuscripts, written under the inspiration of the Holy Spirit, that are considered to be *inerrant*, representing the true Word of God. This same "inerrant" quality can be applied to any accurately made copies or translations of the autographs.

Our culture today places great value upon items that are deemed to be original. Collectors know that an original of anything, be it a painting, a comic book, or a doll, is worth far more than a copy. It seems, however, that God has no interest in such things. In regard to His Word, it appears He is much more concerned with protecting the content than safeguarding the parchment it's written on.

Perishable materials such as papyrus deteriorate rapidly, especially in humid conditions, and have been preserved only in rare instances when the manuscript has been carefully stored in extremely arid climates, such as in Egypt or the Judean desert. Ancient Jewish custodians of the Word of God expected the scrolls and codices (books) to deteriorate over time, so copies were constantly made in order to preserve the contents. There was also the problem of continued use and wear, which would accelerate the damage. Under this scenario, the new scrolls were preferable to the older, worn ones.

Adding to the dilemma of trying to safeguard the originals was the fact that Israel had a lot of enemies. Taking into account the number of wars fought in this particular region over the years, it's a miracle that any manuscripts survived at all. The destruction of the Jewish temple in Jerusalem in 586 BC and again in AD 70 would have put the manuscripts in peril since they were likely stored in the temple library. Priests fleeing the scene would have been concerned about preserving the *content* of the books above all else and therefore would have likely rescued the newer copies.

For this reason, the scribes whose duty it was to copy the Scriptures were charged with making sure they did their job with the utmost accuracy. However, this did not apply to other nonbiblical manuscripts from the ancient world. Therefore, the Old and New Testaments we have today are far more likely to be accurate than other ancient texts such as the *Iliad* by Homer or the works of Aristotle. Famed Jewish historian Josephus reiterated this point just prior to the end of the first century AD when he wrote:

> We have given practical proof of our reverence for our Scriptures. For although such long ages have now passed, no one has ventured to add, or to remove, or to alter a syllable.[3]

Jesus, the apostles, and the Jews of that time period used the *Septuagint*, a Greek translation of the Hebrew Scriptures made in 250 BC, as their Bible. Had there been a problem of inaccuracy, Jesus would have certainly pointed it out, but He didn't. Logic dictates that if God is going to go to the trouble of providing His Word to His people, then He is also going to protect it from significant alterations. Had the preservation of the original autographs been important, He would have taken the necessary steps to guard them. However, God recognized that the accurately made copies were sufficient. It was the content of the message that was important.

There's Gold in Them Hills

In 1947, a treasure trove of ancient Old Testament manuscripts was discovered by a Bedouin goat herder in a cave overlooking the western shore of the Dead Sea in Israel. Over the next few decades, more than 230 texts were found in eleven different caves. Portions of every single book of the Old Testament (except Esther) were represented in what was arguably the greatest manuscript find in history. Some entire books were found, including a perfectly preserved book of Isaiah.[4]

Prior to the discovery of the Dead Sea Scrolls, the earliest known complete text of the Old Testament to survive was the Masoretic manuscript. It was named after the scribal school of the Masoretes whose job was to copy and preserve the texts handed down to them. It is from this manuscript, dated to around the middle of the tenth century AD that most of our English translations of the Old Testament have come. Compiled from a number of medieval sources, the Hebrew Masoretic text was believed to be the most accurate of all surviving Old Testament texts. It has also been the "authorized" version used within Judaism ever since.[5]

For many years, critics had been complaining that the date of the Masoretic text was too late to ensure its accuracy. However, the discovery of the Dead Sea Scrolls silenced such arguments. With some dated as early as 225 BC, these documents were more than one thousand years older than the Masoretic texts![6] And they proved beyond a doubt that the biblical manuscripts had indeed been accurately copied down through the ages. For example, when the books of Isaiah from both sources were compared, it was revealed that 95 percent of the texts were identical. The remaining 5 percent involved only spelling, grammatical, and penmanship differences that did not affect the meaning of the text.[7]

Writer's Cramp

Prior to the invention of the printing press, the only means by which the content of ancient texts could be preserved was, of course, through the painstaking process of copying by hand. Such handwritten copies are used by historians when attempting to authenticate ancient manuscripts when the original autographs haven't survived. The more copies there are and the closer the copies can be dated to the original, the easier it is to validate the accuracy of the manuscript.

Dr. Norman Geisler, professor of theology at Southern Evangelical Seminary, is considered one of the world's leading authorities on the history and accuracy of the Bible. He writes:

> Out of all ancient literature, the New Testament is the most well-authenticated document. There are more manuscripts of the New Testament, plus earlier and more reliable copies of the original manuscripts (autographs) of the New Testament, than any other written work from ancient times.[8]

Specifically, how does the New Testament stack up when compared to other manuscripts from ancient history? Take note of the characteristics of the texts from these well-known early writers ...

The Works of Plato
Date of Manuscript's Origin: 300 BC
Date of Earliest Existing Copy: AD 900
Gap Between Original and Earliest Existing Copy: 1,200 years
Number of Existing Copies: 7

Gallic Wars by Julius Caesar
Date of Manuscript's Origin: 100 BC

Date of Earliest Existing Copy: AD 900

Gap Between Original and Earliest Existing Copy: 1,000 years

Number of Existing Copies: 10

Annals by Tacitus

Date of Manuscript's Origin: AD 100

Date of Earliest Existing Copy: AD 1100

Gap Between Original and Earliest Existing Copy: 1,000 years

Number of Existing Copies: 3

In these examples, notice the length of time between the manuscripts' dates of origin and the dates of the earliest known existing copies, as well as the small number of copies that are known to exist for each. Now compare this information to that of the New Testament texts …

The New Testament

Date of Manuscript's Origin: AD 50–95

Date of Earliest Existing Copy: AD 125

Gap Between Original and Earliest Existing Copy: 30–75 years

Number of Existing Copies: More than 5,700

The validity of the above-cited ancient works of Plato, Caesar, and Tacitus has never been doubted despite the one-thousand-plus-year difference between the originals and the copies, and the small number of copies in existence. On the other hand, the New Testament has less than one hundred years between the writing of the original text and the earliest existing copies, as well as *thousands* of copies to choose from—which virtually guarantees its accuracy. Yet the integrity of the New Testament is impugned on an almost daily basis on many college campuses around the country and in the national media. Professor F. F. Bruce of Manchester University in England writes:

> If the New Testament were a collection of secular writings, their authenticity would generally be regarded as beyond all doubt.[9]

The fact is, if one were to eliminate the New Testament as a viable manuscript, one would have to declare all other ancient texts invalid since no other ancient manuscript even comes close to the authenticity and accuracy of the New Testament. Subsequently, our knowledge of classical history would become … no pun intended … a thing of the past. As Dr. Clark Pinnock of McMaster University in Toronto has penned:

> There exists no document from the ancient world witnessed by so excellent a set of textual and historical testimonies, and offering so superb an array of historical data on which the intelligent decision may be made. An honest person cannot dismiss a source of this kind. Skepticism regarding the historical credentials of Christianity is based upon an irrational bias.[10]

Get It in Writing

For a few years following the resurrection of Jesus, there were no New Testament writings. And yet, the church still grew at a phenomenal pace.

This was made possible through the efforts of the apostles who would travel to different regions and preach to the masses about the resurrected Christ who had fulfilled the Old Testament messianic prophecies. Soon, however, as the needs of the church began to evolve, so too did the methods of teaching.

It quickly became apparent that the oral instruction that took place during the first couple of years would have to expand to include the written Word. Doctrinal questions needed to be clarified. Eyewitness accounts had to be chronicled. Apostles, such as Paul, wanted to find ways to continue to teach while in prison. A written account of what had transpired during the time Jesus was on the earth was required so that the message could carry on beyond the lives of the apostles. And so Matthew, Mark, Luke, John, Paul, James, Peter, and Jude began to write.

A legitimate question would be how and when the various books were chosen for inclusion in the Bible. For the Old Testament, this occurred over a period of one thousand years and concluded during the fifth century BC, when the prophetic activity in Israel came to a halt. Since the first five books of the Old Testament, the Torah, had already been acknowledged as the Word of God, all subsequent books had to conform to them. In addition, short-term prophecies of any potential biblical authors were tested to ensure that they were indeed true prophets of God.[11]

The New Testament Scriptures carried a similar set of requirements for inclusion. First, there could not be any historical or geographical errors. The books had to be written by actual disciples (such as Matthew, John, or Peter) or close associates of Jesus (such as Luke), which limited their authorship to the first century only. And there could be no doctrinal conflicts with the Old Testament.

Contrary to claims from popular Gnostic-themed best sellers such as *The Da Vinci Code*, the books for the New Testament were *not* chosen by

Emperor Constantine for political purposes during the Council of Nicaea in AD 325. The four gospel accounts had already been elevated to the status of "God's Word" (equal to that of the Old Testament) by the end of the second century. The final decision to *canonize* (bring together) the New Testament was made at Carthage in AD 397.[12] The twenty-seven books of the New Testament had already been universally accepted and used regularly by the church for well over two hundred years, and the actions at Carthage merely made it official.

With Every Turn of the Spade ...

During the mid-nineteenth century, a movement began in Germany that would eventually come to be known as the philosophy of higher criticism. Inspired by a number of rationalists from the past, including John Locke, David Hume, and Immanuel Kant, the group, led by theologian David Strauss of the Tubingen school, sought to undermine the Bible and deny the divinity of Jesus Christ.[13] Although Strauss's methodology has since been thoroughly discredited as highly flawed, he was nevertheless able to cause quite a scandal in Europe during that time.[14] Even today, higher criticism's negative impact on Christianity and the reasoning process is still felt.

Famed archeologist Sir William Ramsay was one such individual who had originally bought into the arguments of the Tubingen school of higher criticism. However, the more he began to dig throughout the regions of the Middle East, the more his appreciation for the New Testament texts, which he had originally dismissed as myth, began to grow:

> I began with a mind unfavorable to [Luke's book of Acts], for the ingenuity and apparent completeness of

> the Tubingen theory had at one time quite convinced me.... But more recently I found myself often brought in contact with the book of Acts as an authority for topography, antiquities, and society of Asia Minor. It was gradually borne in upon me that in various details the narrative showed marvelous truth.[15]

Eventually, Ramsay went on to do more than any other archeologist to substantiate the New Testament records as factually and historically accurate (Indiana Jones would be jealous). In particular, Ramsay discovered that Luke was a first-rate historian who had referenced thirty-two countries, fifty-four cities, and nine islands within the text of his gospel and the book of Acts—without a single historical error![16] Other archeologists such as Millar Burrows would come to agree:

> Archeological work has unquestionably strengthened confidence in the reliability of the scriptural record. More than one archeologist has found his respect for the Bible increased by the experience of excavation in Palestine.[17]

As the number of archeological digs began to increase throughout the region of the Middle East during the twentieth century, so too did the number of newly discovered biblical artifacts. By the end of the century there were literally hundreds of thousands of archeological discoveries relating to the Bible.[18] It seemed that with every turn of the archeologist's spade, some portion of the Bible was validated ... or vindicated. Archeologist Nelson Glueck, former student of William F. Albright, the famed pioneer archeologist, concluded:

It may be stated categorically that no archeological discovery has ever controverted a biblical reference. Scores
of archeological findings have been made which confirm
in clear outline or exact detail historical statements in the
Bible.[19]

Proven Reliable

Despite hundreds of thousands of museum pieces and more manuscript
evidence than any other ancient text, some still refuse to accept the Bible
as anything more than a collection of myths. For example, if we were to
ask any number of leading university professors or those in our national
media today if the Bible is reliable, the answer would likely be a resound-
ing "no."

One gentleman who in recent times has had a significant impact
in contributing to the public perception that the Bible isn't worth the
parchment it's written on is "former Christian" Bart Ehrman. Ehrman,
who now claims to be an agnostic, was originally trained at Moody Bible
Institute and Wheaton College in Illinois prior to getting his PhD from
Princeton Theological Seminary. He is currently a professor and chairman of the Department of Religious Studies at the University of North
Carolina and is the author of such books as *The Orthodox Corruption of
Scripture*, *Lost Christianities*, and *Misquoting Jesus*. He believes that the
Bible we have today was so corrupted by the church during the first mil-
lennium that it can no longer be trusted to be an accurate reflection of
history. Ehrman has since gone on to support the Gnostic view of Jesus
as being more valid.[20]

With the release of *Misquoting Jesus* in 2005, Bart Ehrman joined the ranks of the "guest celebrities" and made the media rounds in order to promote his work, appearing on a number of TV channels including CNN, NBC, A&E, the Discovery Channel, the History Channel, and National Geographic. One such book tour culminated with an appearance on *The Daily Show* with Jon Stewart, where he was congratulated on his efforts to expose "the deliberate corruption of the Scriptures," which made the Bible seem, at least to the host, *"more interesting ... almost more godly in some respects."*[21] Within forty-eight hours of the airing of the program, *Misquoting Jesus* had risen to the number-one position on the Amazon.com Web site and solidified its *New York Times* best-seller status, thereby becoming "one of the unlikeliest best sellers of the year."[22]

Around the same time, author and mystic Michael Baigent began popping up on a number of similar programs, including *Dateline NBC* and *The Today Show*, promoting his latest book, *The Jesus Papers*.[23] His previous attempt to undermine the Bible, a work titled *Holy Blood, Holy Grail*, had served as the inspiration for *The Da Vinci Code* by Dan Brown without his permission (in fact, the two men were embroiled in a legal battle just as the big-budget film version of Brown's thriller was about to hit the theaters).[24] As the following exchange with *Dateline* correspondent Sara James reveals, Baigent was quite open about the real agenda behind the writing of his book:

Sara James, Dateline correspondent: You believe that much of what we think we know about Jesus is a lie?

Michael Baigent, author: It's a lie. It's an obvious lie.

James: So basically, you're asking anybody who is a Christian to question their fundamental beliefs?

Baigent: Absolutely.

James: Some might call your position heresy.

Baigent: I should hope they would.[25]

Do such claims have any validity? Before believers feel the urge to renounce their faith, they should recognize that the basic theology and biases of critics like Ehrman and Baigent can easily be shown to be suspect (see chapter 8). The scholarship behind both of these men's work has been called into question by historians who have examined their writings.[26]

One scholar who has scrutinized such claims under a microscope is Randall Price, PhD, ThM, professor of Jewish studies at Liberty University and professor of archeology and biblical history at Trinity Southwest University. Price sees the current barrage of criticisms leveled at the Bible as a blessing in disguise which has forced historians to ensure that the Scriptures we have today are as demonstratively accurate as possible:

> The work of textual critics today is bringing us ever closer to the Original Bible. Despite the thousands of translations made ... the text has remained essentially unchanged. And certainly nothing that affects doctrine or practice has been lost or altered through thousands of years of the history of textual transmission. This is a conviction that can be maintained even in the current marketplace of ideas, where skepticism reigns and the integrity of the Bible is daily maligned in the media.[27]

Mind-set Lament

The German school of higher criticism has been impacting Western culture for more than a century and a half. Many if not most of our university, college, and even seminary professors today have been influenced by it to one degree or another and have in turn influenced their millions of students. The results have been an intense yet unnecessary distrust of the Judeo-Christian Scriptures among members of the general populace.

While we await the appearance of any fabled "mountain of evidence that can prove the Bible wrong," there is something that could ultimately turn out to be far more problematic—a new way of thinking which has been emerging for decades ... where truth is relative and evidence doesn't really matter all that much. Dr. Craig Evans, author and director of the graduate program at Acadia Divinity College in Nova Scotia, laments that it is precisely because of this mind-set that so many antibiblical books in recent years have become best sellers within our popular culture:

> Our postmodern, irrational society, where truth is subjective and negotiable, probably has something to do with it. As one reviewer put it: The success of *The Da Vinci Code* says more about the gullibility of modern society than it does about Dan Brown's skills.[28]

Countless numbers of Gnostic promoters, media pundits, and university professors today clamor for us to relegate the Bible to the scrap heap. Many Christians believe that such a request needs to be countered in an effective manner—and the sooner the better. Professor of archeology Randall Price feels the timing couldn't be more critical:

If attacks on the integrity of the biblical texts continue
to erode their long-standing status as Scripture, they will
discredit the Bible's authority for the general population,
including the majority of the Christian community. And
if, subsequently, the heretical doctrines and values of an
alternate Christianity are accepted, the ultimate result
could be the collapse of Western Culture, which has been
built upon the Scripture. However, this would be followed
not by a lack of religion, but by a new dominance of other
religions—those that have been waiting in the wings.[29]

With each passing day, I continue to be amazed by the manner in
which the very people who like to be called "scholars" reject the most well-
documented book in the world and simultaneously refuse to acknowledge
the most influential person who has ever lived. These same people then
turn around and accept the flimsiest of unauthenticated documents,
such as those of the Gnostics, which often contradict history and sound
reasoning. Early twentieth-century English writer G. K. Chesterton best
summed up the dilemma when he wrote:

It's the first effect of not believing in God that you lose
your common sense.[30]

Chapter Three

ALL SIGNS POINT HIS WAY

Prophets who rely on the supernatural realm for their wisdom can be divided into two basic groups—those who prophesy in the name of the creator God as illustrated by the Hebrew prophets whose predictions were recorded in the Bible; and those who receive their information as a result of practicing various forms of sorcery.

Madame Helena Blavatsky is one such individual who falls into the second camp. She was an influential nineteenth-century occultist who founded the Theosophical Society, an organization that eventually served as the foundation for the New Age movement in the 1980s. Her abilities of clairvoyance and channeling, which allowed extradimensional entities to speak through her, resulted in the creation of a massive series of books including *Isis Unveiled* and *The Secret Doctrine.*[1]

Edgar Cayce, commonly referred to as the sleeping prophet, was an American psychic who lived during the first half of the twentieth century. He frequently taught while in a hypnotic trance on subjects such as reincarnation, astrology, and the existence of the lost city of Atlantis.

Perhaps the most well known of these types of prophets was a gentleman by the name of Michel de Nostredame, better known as Nostradamus, the prophet of doom. Born in 1503 in the south of France, his fame quickly spread throughout Europe following the 1555 publication of his book titled *Les Propheties*. The book has remained hugely popular to this day and has resulted in Nostradamus's large, almost cultlike following the world over. Skeptics of Nostradamus are quick to point out that his reputation as a prophet has been largely manufactured by modern-day supporters who match his vague and often cryptic writings to events after they occur. In fact, his critics contend his writings are so tenuous that they remain essentially useless in trying to predict any event in advance with even the smallest degree of certainty. This has prompted the wry observation that *Nostradamus is 100 percent accurate at predicting events after they happen.*[2]

Speaking of being 100 percent accurate, biblical prophets were in fact required to be just that ... 100 percent accurate in all of their predictions; and if they failed to measure up—for example, get just one prophecy wrong out of one thousand—they would be condemned as false and subsequently executed!

> But the prophet who presumes to speak a word in My name, which I have not commanded him to speak, or who speaks in the name of other gods, that prophet shall die. And if you say in your heart, 'How shall we know the word which the LORD has not spoken?'—when a prophet speaks in the name of the LORD, if the thing does not happen or come to pass, that is the thing which the LORD has not spoken; the prophet has spoken it presumptuously; you shall not be afraid of him. (Deuteronomy 18:20–22)

The Prophetic Word

More than one fourth of the Bible's content was prophetic at the time that it was originally written. To date, more than half of these one-thousand-plus prophecies have been fulfilled down to the minutest of details. With its track record of 100 percent accuracy, we can be confident that the remainder of the Bible's yet-to-be-fulfilled prophecies, including those dealing with the *last days* and beyond, will no doubt come to pass in due time. Since the fulfilled prophecies have come to fruition in a literal as opposed to a symbolic or allegorical manner, we have an intellectual basis for believing that those prophecies that are yet future will likewise be fulfilled literally.

> Remember the former things of old, for I am God, and there is no other; *I am God, and there is none like Me, declaring the end from the beginning, and from ancient times things that are not yet done,* saying, "My counsel shall stand, and I will do all My pleasure." (Isaiah 46:9–10)

It is ironic and unfortunate that a number of Bible teachers in recent years have failed to recognize the undeniable importance of prophecy, especially when one realizes that *fulfilled prophecy validates the Bible itself.* Since all of the fulfilled biblical prophecies have proven to be meticulously precise and accurate throughout the centuries, it stands to reason that what the Bible has to say about other things—such as the attributes of God, specifics about the creation, and the existence of heaven and hell—are 100 percent accurate as well. It also stands to reason that the Bible's content is not man-made but instead has its origins outside of our own space-time continuum, because *it records history before it happens.* In essence, prophecy is history written in advance.

More than seventy prophets are named within the pages of the Bible. Abraham, Moses, David, Elijah, Isaiah, Jeremiah, Ezekiel, Daniel, John the Baptist, and even Jesus Himself are just a few of the more prominent ones. Their prophecies cover just about every topic imaginable—from the rise and fall of leaders, to the fate of the world's nations, to specific details involving the Messiah.

World Dictators Need Not Apply

One of the more remarkable prophecies in the Bible can be found in the second chapter of the book of Daniel. The prophet Daniel was asked to recall King Nebuchadnezzar's dream that the Babylonian soothsayers, astrologers, magicians, and false prophets had been unable to do. Undaunted, Daniel relied on the *God in heaven who reveals secrets* (Daniel 2:28) to help him not only recall the dream, but interpret its meaning as well. The interpretation turned out to be a prophecy describing the four future empires that would eventually rule the entire world. These included the Babylonians, followed by the Medo-Persians, the Greeks, and finally the Romans. Here, Daniel, standing before King Nebuchadnezzar of Babylon, tells him of the kingdoms which are to come:

> You, O king, are a king of kings. For the God of heaven has given you a kingdom, power, strength, and glory; and wherever the children of men dwell, or the beasts of the field and the birds of the heaven, He has given them into your hand, and has made you ruler over them all—you are this head of gold. But after you shall arise another kingdom inferior to yours; then another, a third kingdom

of bronze, which shall rule over all the earth. And the fourth kingdom shall be as strong as iron, inasmuch as iron breaks in pieces and shatters everything; and like iron that crushes, that kingdom will break in pieces and crush all the others. (Daniel 2:37–40)

Additional information about these world empires, including their specific identities, appears throughout the book of Daniel. These prophecies are so accurate that many scoffers insist the book of Daniel must have been written after the fact. In reality, no other book of the Bible has been attacked and maligned by its opponents with such ferocity over the years. These critics claim the book was most likely penned sometime during the second century since it would have been impossible for anyone to have predicted the events of these future world kingdoms, which didn't even exist at the time, with such detail.[3] However, such allegations have recently begun to fade. The skeptics suffered a heavy setback when Daniel's manuscripts were found in the caves of Qumran as part of the historic Dead Sea Scrolls discovery. In fact, Daniel's documents represented the second-largest number of major prophet texts found at Qumran—second only to those of Isaiah.[4]

It is now evident from the findings at Qumran that no canonical writing can be dated later than the end of the Persian period, i.e., much beyond 350 B.C.[5]

What this means is that the latest possible date that the book of Daniel (or any other Old Testament manuscript) can be assigned is 350 BC—which is still early enough for all of the prophecies to be legitimate. Their fulfillment simply serves to reinforce the divine inspiration behind the Scriptures.

What is assuring to us in the twenty-first century is that in the last twenty-five hundred years, there have only been four world empires—the Babylonians, the Medo-Persians, the Greeks, and the Romans—exactly as the prophet Daniel predicted there would be. Many other potential dictators with their sights set on controlling the world have appeared on the scene since the time of Theodosius, the last of the Roman emperors to rule over a unified Rome. Yet the grand schemes of world conquest of the Genghis Khans, the Napoleon Bonapartes, the Adolph Hitlers, and the Joseph Stalins have always ended in failure. The prophetic words of Daniel stated there would be only four world empires … and, just as predicted, there have been only four. From a human perspective, how could Daniel possibly have known this so many centuries in advance?

> Knowing this first, that no prophecy of Scripture is of
> any private interpretation, for prophecy never came by
> the will of man, but holy men of God spoke as they were
> moved by the Holy Spirit. (2 Peter 1:20–21)

By the 1990s, with archeological evidence continuing to mount, skeptics had pretty much lost hope of trying to date the Old Testament Scriptures any later than the generally accepted date of origin. A *Time* magazine article from 1995 conceded that modern archeological information had "strengthened the Bible's claim to historical accuracy" as well as early composition[6] (one of the few times this magazine had something positive to say about the Bible). As one small example, the author referenced two silver scrolls that had been discovered in a tomb in Jerusalem:

> They were dated around 600 B.C., shortly before the
> destruction of Solomon's Temple and the Israelites' exile

in Babylon. When scientists carefully unrolled the scrolls at the Israel Museum, they found a benediction from the Book of Numbers etched into their surface. The discovery made it clear that parts of the Old Testament were being copied long before some skeptics had believed they were even written.[7]

Anticipating the Messiah

By far, the most important topic of Old Testament prophecy involves the appearance of the Messiah. More than anything else, God seemed to want to let people know ahead of time as much as He could about the Messiah, including how, when, and where He would appear on earth. To those whose minds were open to receive such information, the effects of the prophecies were indeed life changing. The gospel of Luke, for example, records how Simeon anticipated the arrival of the Messiah based on his understanding of the Old Testament Scriptures. Not coincidentally, he arrived at the temple in Jerusalem at the very moment Joseph and Mary brought the infant Jesus to the temple for the first time.

> And behold, there was a man in Jerusalem whose name was Simeon, and this man was just and devout, waiting for the Consolation of Israel, and the Holy Spirit was upon him. And it had been revealed to him by the Holy Spirit that he would not see death before he had seen the Lord's Christ. So he came by the Spirit into the temple. And when the parents brought in the Child Jesus, to do

for Him according to the custom of the law, he took Him
up in his arms and blessed God and said: "Lord, now
You are letting Your servant depart in peace, according to
Your word; for my eyes have seen Your salvation which
You have prepared before the face of all peoples, a light
to bring revelation to the Gentiles, and the glory of Your
people Israel." (Luke 2:25–32)

Sadly, the religious leaders of the day completely missed the boat. The
very group who more than any other should have recognized the appearance of the Messiah because of their "knowledge" of the Scriptures refused
to accept Him. In fact, when Jesus arrived on the scene years later as an
adult, they were quite hostile to say the least. And it wasn't simply a lack
of knowledge or unfamiliarity with the Scriptures that was the problem.
For them, it was a matter of the heart, not the head. In addressing these
religious leaders Jesus stated:

But you do not have His word abiding in you, because
whom He sent, Him you do not believe. (John 5:38)

Prophecies Fulfilled

In his book titled *The Life and Times of Jesus the Messiah*, nineteenth-
century author Alfred Edersheim claimed to have found 456 messianic
passages in the Old Testament. If we eliminate the repetitive ones, we
are still left with over one hundred distinct prophecies that describe in
detail the coming Messiah's initial appearance on the earth.[8] Jesus Christ,
of course, fulfilled them all.

The Messiah's Virgin Birth

The first prophecy in the Bible can be found right near the beginning, in the third chapter of the book of Genesis, and foretells a unique aspect of the birth of the Messiah ...

> So the LORD God said to the serpent: "Because you have done this, you are cursed more than all cattle, and more than every beast of the field; on your belly you shall go, and you shall eat dust all the days of your life. And I will put enmity between you and the woman, and between your seed and her Seed. (Genesis 3:14–15)

The reference to the future Messiah coming from "the seed of the woman" has been accepted by rabbis and scholars down through the ages to mean that He would be born of a virgin.

> Therefore the Lord Himself will give you a sign: Behold, the virgin shall conceive and bear a Son, and shall call His name Immanuel. (Isaiah 7:14)

As we all know, people are conceived utilizing the egg from the mother and the sperm (seed) from the father. But the New Testament gospels make it clear that Jesus had no human father—the seed was planted within Mary miraculously by the Holy Spirit. Therefore, we have the unusual reference to "her Seed" in Genesis. (Incidentally, this has caused some theologians to conclude that the "gene" for sin is passed down from the male of our species. Since Jesus was conceived without a human father, it might explain how the fully human Mary could give birth to a sinless Messiah. Others, such as medical doctor M. R. DeHaan, believe that God provided *both* the egg and the sperm for the future Messiah, thus rendering

Mary as the "incubator" or "surrogate mother" who would provide life and nourishment to Jesus as He grew within her. In either case, Jesus would be born without the taint of the Adamic nature and could therefore atone for the sins of the world with His sinless blood.)

Matthew's documentation of the virgin birth of Jesus clearly identifies it as the fulfillment of Isaiah's prophecy written seven hundred years earlier:

> Now the birth of Jesus Christ was as follows: After His mother Mary was betrothed to Joseph, before they came together, she was found with child of the Holy Spirit. Then Joseph her husband, being a just man, and not wanting to make her a public example, was minded to put her away secretly. But while he thought about these things, behold, an angel of the Lord appeared to him in a dream, saying, "Joseph, son of David, do not be afraid to take to you Mary your wife, for that which is conceived in her is of the Holy Spirit. And she will bring forth a Son, and you shall call His name JESUS, for He will save His people from their sins." So all this was done that it might be fulfilled which was spoken by the Lord through the prophet, saying: "Behold, the virgin shall be with child, and bear a Son, and they shall call His name Immanuel," which is translated, "God with us." (Matthew 1:18–23)

The Messiah's Genealogy

Numerous prophecies in the Old Testament foretell the genealogical lineage from which the Messiah would eventually come. These messianic ancestors include Shem (Genesis 11:10), Abraham (Genesis 12:7), Isaac

(Genesis 17:19), Jacob (Genesis 28:13), Judah (Genesis 49:10), and David (Isaiah 9:7), to name only a few. It should be understood that the potential candidates for the Messiah narrowed with each succeeding generation until we were left with Jesus as the only one who was able to fulfill all of the genealogical prophecies. The family history of Jesus is confirmed in the first chapter of the book of Matthew (Joseph's side) and the third chapter of the book of Luke (Mary's side).

The Messiah's Birth in Bethlehem

The prophet Micah predicted that the Messiah would be born in the small town of Bethlehem:

> But you, Bethlehem Ephrathah, though you are little among the thousands of Judah, yet out of you shall come forth to Me the One to be Ruler in Israel, whose goings forth are from of old, from everlasting. (Micah 5:2)

Joseph and Mary did not live in Bethlehem but were forced to travel there as required by the tax laws just as she was about to give birth. The fact that Mary, while most likely either walking or riding on a donkey, did not go into labor during the grueling ninety-mile journey over rough terrain was a miracle in itself! The second chapter of both Matthew's and Luke's gospels confirm that Jesus was indeed born in Bethlehem:

> Now after Jesus was born in Bethlehem of Judea in the days of Herod the king, behold, wise men from the East came to Jerusalem, saying, "Where is He who has been born King of the Jews? For we have seen His star in the

East and have come to worship Him." When Herod
the king heard this, he was troubled, and all Jerusalem
with him. And when he had gathered all the chief priests
and scribes of the people together, he inquired of them
where the Christ was to be born. So they said to him, "In
Bethlehem of Judea, for thus it is written by the prophet:
'But you, Bethlehem, in the land of Judah, are not the
least among the rulers of Judah; for out of you shall come
a Ruler who will shepherd My people Israel.'" (Matthew
2:1–6)

The Messiah's Exit from Egypt

In addition to His prophesied birth in Bethlehem, another curious prediction implied that the Messiah would also come out of Egypt:

> "When Israel was a child, I loved him, and out of Egypt
> I called My son." (Hosea 11:1)

God's warning to Joseph to quickly take his wife and newborn Son
to Egypt not only saved Jesus' life, but simultaneously fulfilled Hosea's
prophecy:

> An angel of the Lord appeared to Joseph in a dream,
> saying, "Arise, take the young Child and His mother,
> flee to Egypt, and stay there until I bring you word;
> for Herod will seek the young Child to destroy Him."
> When he arose, he took the young Child and His
> mother by night and departed for Egypt, and was there

until the death of Herod, that it might be fulfilled which was spoken by the Lord through the prophet, saying, "Out of Egypt I called My Son." Then Herod, when he saw that he was deceived by the wise men, was exceedingly angry; and he sent forth and put to death all the male children who were in Bethlehem and in all its districts, from two years old and under, according to the time which he had determined from the wise men. Then was fulfilled what was spoken by Jeremiah the prophet, saying: "A voice was heard in Ramah, lamentation, weeping, and great mourning, Rachel weeping for her children, refusing to be comforted, because they are no more." (Matthew 2:13–18)

Incredibly, this section of the second chapter of Matthew records the fulfillment of three major prophecies: (1) the Messiah being born in Bethlehem, (2) the Messiah being called out of Egypt, and (3) the intense mourning in the land resulting from the loss of innocent life due to King Herod's order to kill all male children two years of age and younger.

The Messiah's Forerunner

Two Hebrew prophets, Isaiah and Malachi, both prophesied that there would be a forerunner to the Messiah—someone who would prepare the way and announce to the world that the Messiah was about to appear. That role was filled by the man known as John the Baptist.

Incidentally, part of the judgment of God against Israel due to their apostasy was to remove the prophetic voice from their prophets. Consequently, Israel would not hear from God via a prophet for four hundred years (hence the four-hundred-year gap between the Old and New Testaments). One reason behind the Israelites' ready acceptance of John the Baptist was to fill this spiritual void. When John entered the world preaching repentance and baptism, thousands flocked to him as a prophet of God:

> Behold, I send My messenger, and he will prepare the way before Me. (Malachi 3:1)

> The voice of one crying in the wilderness: "Prepare the way of the LORD; make straight in the desert a highway for our God. Every valley shall be exalted and every mountain and hill brought low; the crooked places shall be made straight and the rough places smooth; the glory of the LORD shall be revealed, and all flesh shall see it together; for the mouth of the LORD has spoken." (Isaiah 40:3–5)

Luke's gospel records the fulfillment of Isaiah's prophecy by identifying John the Baptist as the "voice of one crying in the wilderness" …

> The word of God came to John the son of Zacharias in the wilderness. And he went into all the region around the Jordan, preaching a baptism of repentance for the remission of sins, as it is written in the book of the words of Isaiah the prophet, saying: "The voice of one crying in the wilderness: 'Prepare the way of the LORD; make His paths straight. Every valley shall be filled and every mountain and hill brought low; the crooked places shall be made

straight and the rough ways smooth; and all flesh shall see
the salvation of God.'" (Luke 3:2–6)

John was regarded highly, not only by those who knew of him, but
by Jesus Himself, who identified the Baptist as the fulfillment of Malachi's
prophecy:

> Jesus began to say to the multitudes concerning John:
> "What did you go out into the wilderness to see?... A
> prophet? Yes, I say to you, and more than a prophet.
> For this is he of whom it is written: 'Behold, I send My
> messenger before Your face, who will prepare Your way
> before You.' Assuredly, I say to you, among those born
> of women there has not risen one greater than John the
> Baptist." (Matthew 11:7, 9–11)

The Messiah's Presentation of Himself to Israel

Almost six hundred years before Jesus was born, the prophet Daniel gave
us an indication of when the Messiah would appear on the earth:

> Seventy weeks are determined for your people and for your
> holy city, to finish the transgression, to make an end of
> sins, to make reconciliation for iniquity, to bring in ever-
> lasting righteousness, to seal up vision and prophecy, and
> to anoint the Most Holy. Know therefore and understand,
> that from the going forth of the command to restore and
> build Jerusalem until Messiah the Prince, there shall be
> seven weeks and sixty-two weeks. (Daniel 9:24–25)

With a little bit of detective work, this important prophecy can be easily unraveled. The Hebrew term "heptads" translated here as *weeks* is a numerical term that literally means *units of seven*, which is similar to our English words "pair" meaning *two* or "dozen" meaning *twelve*. The context makes it clear that we are referring to a specific number of years in regards to these "units of seven" ... sixty-nine to be exact, which we arrive at by adding seven to sixty-two. Sixty-nine units of seven years equal 483 years. The decree to rebuild Jerusalem referenced in this prophecy was given by Artaxerxes in 444 BC (see Nehemiah chapter 2). By utilizing the standard 360-day Hebrew calendar, we can determine that the prophesied Messiah would have had to appear no later than the year AD 33—which is the very time Jesus was crucified in Jerusalem! This prophecy makes it clear there simply is no other logical candidate for the Hebrew Messiah than Jesus of Nazareth.

It gets even better. A week before the crucifixion, Jesus rode into Jerusalem on a donkey and presented Himself to Israel as their Messiah just as the prophet Zechariah predicted He would:

> Rejoice greatly, O daughter of Zion! Shout, O daughter
> of Jerusalem! Behold, your King is coming to you; He is
> just and having salvation, lowly and riding on a donkey,
> a colt, the foal of a donkey. (Zechariah 9:9)

The eleventh chapter of Mark's gospel identifies Zechariah's prophecy as being fulfilled on this particular afternoon which, as it turns out, was *483 years to the day* after Artaxerxes gave the decree to rebuild Jerusalem!

Daniel's complete prophecy calls for a total of seventy units of seven or 490 years with a break between the sixty-ninth and seventieth unit, which leaves one seven-year period still unaccounted for. Since the first 483 years were fulfilled historically, we can expect the last seven years also to be fulfilled historically. The final seven-year period to come is designated the tribulation, referenced forty-nine times by the Hebrew prophets and described in detail in the book of Revelation. And just as the first 483-year period concluded with the Messiah's triumphant entry into Jerusalem, so too will the last seven-year period conclude with the second coming of Christ![9]

The Messiah's Betrayal

There are many prophecies in the Old Testament concerning the Messiah's betrayal, His silence before His accusers, His execution, His burial, and His resurrection. Jesus was of course familiar with them and knew from the beginning that it was His destiny for all of them to be fulfilled. Most of these prophecies are incredibly specific. Take for example those that revolve around the betrayal of Jesus by his own friend and disciple Judas:

The Prophecy:

Even my own familiar friend in whom I trusted, who ate my bread, has lifted up his heel against me. (Psalm 41:9)

The Fulfillment:

Jesus answered, "It is he to whom I shall give a piece of bread when I have dipped it." And having dipped the bread, He gave it to Judas Iscariot, the son of Simon. (John 13:26)

The Prophecy:

Then I said to them, "If it is agreeable to you, give me my wages; and if not, refrain." So they weighed out for my wages thirty pieces of silver. (Zechariah 11:12)

The Fulfillment:

Then one of the twelve, called Judas Iscariot, went to the chief priests and said, "What are you willing to give me if I deliver Him to you?" And they counted out to him thirty pieces of silver. (Matthew 26:14–15)

The Prophecy:

And the Lord said to me, "Throw it to the potter"—that princely price they set on me. So I took the thirty pieces of silver and threw them into the house of the Lord for the potter. (Zechariah 11:13)

The Fulfillment:

Then Judas, His betrayer, seeing that He had been condemned, was remorseful and brought back the thirty pieces of silver to the chief priests and elders, saying, "I have sinned by betraying innocent blood." And they said, "What is that to us? You see to it!" Then he threw down the pieces of silver in the temple and departed, and went and hanged himself. But the chief priests took the silver pieces and said, "It is not lawful to put them into the treasury, because they are the price of blood." And they consulted together and bought with them the potter's field, to bury strangers in. (Matthew 27:3–7)

The Messiah's Silence

The Prophecy:

He was oppressed and He was afflicted, yet He opened not His mouth; He was led as a lamb to the slaughter, and as a sheep before its shearers is silent, so He opened not His mouth. (Isaiah 53:7)

The Fulfillment:

And while He [Jesus] was being accused by the chief priests and elders, He answered nothing. Then Pilate said to Him, "Do You not hear how many things they testify against You?" But He answered him not one word. (Matthew 27:12–14)

The Messiah's Crucifixion

The Prophecy:

And I will pour on the house of David and on the inhabitants of Jerusalem the Spirit of grace and supplication; then they will look on Me whom they pierced. Yes, they will mourn for Him as one mourns for his only son, and grieve for Him as one grieves for a firstborn. (Zechariah 12:10)

The Fulfillment:

But one of the soldiers pierced His side with a spear, and immediately blood and water came out. (John 19:34)

The Prophecy:

They divide My garments among them, and for My clothing they cast lots. (Psalm 22:18)

The Fulfillment:

Then they crucified Him, and divided His garments, casting lots, that it might be fulfilled which was spoken by the prophet: "They divided My garments among them, and for My clothing they cast lots." (Matthew 27:35)

The Prophecy:

My God, My God, why have You forsaken Me? Why are You so far from helping Me, and from the words of My groaning? (Psalm 22:1)

The Fulfillment:

And about the ninth hour Jesus cried out with a loud voice, saying, "Eli, Eli, lama sabachthani?" that is, "My God, My God, why have You forsaken Me?" (Matthew 27:46)

The Prophecy:

He guards all his bones; not one of them is broken. (Psalm 34:20)

The Fulfillment:

Then the soldiers came and broke the legs of the first and of the other who was crucified with Him. But when they came to Jesus and saw that He was already dead, they did not break His legs. (John 19:32–33)

The Messiah's Burial

The Prophecy:

And they made His grave with the wicked—but with the rich at His death, because He had done no violence, nor was any deceit in His mouth. (Isaiah 53:9)

The Fulfillment:

Now when evening had come, there came a rich man from Arimathea, named Joseph, who himself had also become a disciple of Jesus. This man went to Pilate and asked for the body of Jesus. Then Pilate commanded the body to be given to him. When Joseph had taken the body, he wrapped it in a clean linen cloth, and laid it in his new tomb which he had hewn out of the rock; and he rolled a large stone against the door of the tomb, and departed. (Matthew 27:57–60)

The Messiah's Resurrection

The Prophecy:

For You will not leave my soul in Sheol, nor will You allow Your Holy One to see corruption. (Psalm 16:10)

The Fulfillment:

> He [David], foreseeing this, spoke concerning the resur-
> rection of the Christ, that His soul was not left in Hades,
> nor did His flesh see corruption. This Jesus God has raised
> up, of which we are all witnesses. (Acts 2:31–32)

Following His resurrection, Jesus met up with two men walking along the road headed toward the village of Emmaus. Although the men did not recognize Jesus at first, they were quite familiar with the events that had led up to the crucifixion of a man who had turned Jerusalem upside down during the previous three and a half years. Using Old Testament Scriptures, Jesus was able to prove to them that the man who had been crucified was indeed the prophesied Messiah. And it wasn't until after Jesus had left their midst that the men realized they had been talking with the risen Messiah Himself the entire time.[10]

Could He Be a Fraud?

These examples are only a handful of the more than one hundred messianic prophecies Jesus fulfilled during His lifetime. For centuries, skeptics, rationalists, scoffers, and secularists have tried to dismiss such claims as coincidental or even fraudulent, since the idea of fulfilled prophecy contradicts their *natural* view of the world. And as we will be examining in chapter 8 of this book, those of the Gnostic persuasion have created a cottage industry out of devising some of the most ingenious conspiracy theories imaginable in order to try to strip Jesus of any possible claim to deity or messiahship.

Nevertheless, the sincere seeker of truth should not be afraid to examine the question of whether or not Jesus was a fraud. Is it possible Jesus could have *force-fulfilled over one hundred prophecies* in order to make Himself appear to be the Messiah?

I suppose it is conceivable (although clearly out of character) that everyone involved in confirming the virgin birth could have lied. On the other hand, Jesus could not have manipulated His ancestral history, His birth in Bethlehem, or His journey to Egypt as an infant in order to fulfill those prophecies. Jesus *could* have prearranged His triumphant entry into the city of Jerusalem on the back of a donkey on the exact day necessary to coincide with Daniel's and Zechariah's prophecies. However, He could not have engineered His birth in order to guarantee He would be alive during the proper time period in history to fulfill such a prophecy.

Jesus wasn't even present while the prophecies involving the payment to Judas were unfolding. And it would have been illogical for Judas (working in collusion with the chief priests, no less!) to fulfill these extremely specific prophecies for the benefit of a man he was in the process of betraying.

Although Jesus could have cried out the words of the psalmist while hanging on the cross in order to force-fulfill the prophecy confirmed in Matthew 27:46, He would have had a difficult time manipulating the piercing of His side, the gambling for His clothes, and the timing of His death in order to avoid the breaking of His legs. And is it logical to believe that someone who is in such agony would be concerned with meticulously fulfilling a myriad of ancient prophecies (for fraudulent purposes) while He was in the process of dying an excruciating death?

Finally, Jesus had many enemies during the time He was on the earth and a lot of these enemies had a working knowledge of Old Testament

Scriptures. All they would have needed to do is keep Jesus from fulfilling *just one* prophecy and He would have automatically been disqualified as the Messiah. However, no one was able to do that.

What Are the Odds?

What are the mathematical odds of one man either fulfilling by chance or through manipulation over one hundred prophecies written hundreds of years before his birth? Professor and mathematician Peter Stoner wondered himself. Stoner was chairman of the Departments of Mathematics and Astronomy at Pasadena City College in California for many years before becoming professor emeritus of science at Westmont College. He calculated the mathematical probabilities of one man fulfilling a portion of the messianic prophecies and released his research results in a publication titled *Science Speaks: Scientific Proof of the Accuracy of Prophecy and the Bible*.

Stoner concluded that the probability of one person fulfilling just eight messianic prophecies was 1 in 10 to the 17th power, or 100,000,000,000,000,000 to 1. He then calculated the odds of someone fulfilling 48 of these prophecies to be 1 in 10 to the 157th power, or 10,000,000,000,000,000,000,000,000,000,000,000,000,000,000,000, 000,000,000,000,000,000,000,000,000,000,000,000,000,000,000,000, 000,000,000,000,000,000,000,000,000,000,000,000,000,000,000,000, 000,000,000,000,000 to 1.[11] Such a number is so large as to be incomprehensible.

If we base our belief solely on the science of mathematical probabilities, Jesus Christ becomes, without question, the prophesied Messiah of the Old Testament.

Looking toward the Future

In addition to the prophecies that indicate the Messiah would suffer and die for the sins of all people, a number of prophecies also identify Him as a king destined to rule over the governments of the world.

> And behold, One like the Son of Man, coming with the clouds of heaven! He came to the Ancient of Days, and they brought Him near before Him. Then to Him was given dominion and glory and a kingdom, that all peoples, nations, and languages should serve Him. His dominion is an everlasting dominion, which shall not pass away, and His kingdom the one which shall not be destroyed. (Daniel 7:13–14)

Based on the chronicles of Jesus' life as recorded in the Gospels, it's clear He did not fulfill any "kingly" prophecies during His first appearance on the earth. These are part of the group of yet-to-be-fulfilled prophecies that will come to pass during *His second coming and subsequent millennial and eternal kingdoms.* Contributing to the potential confusion, many Old Testament messianic prophecies include references to both *the suffering servant* and *the ruling king* within the same passage with no mention of any time interval separating the two:

> For unto us a Child is born, unto us a Son is given; and the government will be upon His shoulder. And His name will be called Wonderful, Counselor, Mighty God, Everlasting Father, Prince of Peace. Of the increase of His government and peace there will be no end, upon the throne of David and over His kingdom, to order it

and establish it with judgment and justice from that time
forward, even forever. (Isaiah 9:6–7)

To fully understand these prophecies we must realize that the
Messiah was destined to make two distinct appearances on the earth:
the first time to sacrifice Himself for the sins of the world and the
second time to rule and reign as heir to David's throne. In the example
above, the first part of the prophecy refers to His first coming (a Child
is born, a Son is given) and the remainder of the passage refers to His
second coming.

The religious leaders of Jesus' day did not want a martyred Savior who
would save them from their sins. They demanded a king who would over-
throw the controlling government immediately and rule over the nations.
They didn't realize they needed to be cleansed of their sins first, along with
the rest of the world. Only when Jesus returns to the earth during the *last days*
in power and glory will the rest of the prophecies identifying the Messiah as
king be fulfilled.

One extremely interesting prophecy from Zechariah quoted earlier in
this chapter depicts the ruling Messiah as the protector of Jerusalem who
will destroy those nations who come against her. But notice there is also
a reference to the crucifixion, proving that the future ruling Messiah and
crucified Messiah are, of course, one and the same.

> It shall be in that day that I will seek to destroy all the
> nations that come against Jerusalem. And I will pour on
> the house of David and on the inhabitants of Jerusalem
> the Spirit of grace and supplication; then they will look
> on Me whom they pierced. Yes, they will mourn for Him
> as one mourns for his only son, and grieve for Him as one
> grieves for a firstborn. (Zechariah 12:9–10)

This is why every serious seeker after truth should make a determined effort to study biblical prophecy. Because the religious leaders who were in charge during the time of Christ did not fully understand the prophetic Scriptures, they failed to recognize Jesus as the Messiah when He appeared on earth the first time. Today, as we move ever closer toward the *last days*, those who have rejected the study of prophecy will likewise be unprepared for Jesus' second coming.

Chapter Four

WHO ELSE CAN DO THESE THINGS?

Old Testament prophecies portrayed the coming Messiah as someone who would be capable of performing astonishing miracles. These "signs" would subsequently validate to eyewitnesses that they were indeed in the presence of the Messiah. More than anything else, the miracles of Jesus Christ proved beyond any doubt that He was indeed who He claimed to be—the Son of God.

> "Behold, your God will come with vengeance, with the recompense of God; He will come and save you." Then the eyes of the blind shall be opened, and the ears of the deaf shall be unstopped. Then the lame shall leap like a deer, and the tongue of the dumb sing. (Isaiah 35:4–6)

He Healed Them All

The New Testament documents nearly forty different instances of Jesus performing some type of miracle. However, the individual miracles actually performed probably numbered in the thousands during His short three-and-a-half-year ministry. Obviously, no case was too difficult for Him:

> And He came down with them and stood on a level place with a crowd of His disciples and a great multitude of people from all Judea and Jerusalem, and from the seacoast of Tyre and Sidon, who came to hear Him and be healed of their diseases, as well as those who were tormented with unclean spirits. And they were healed. And the whole multitude sought to touch Him, for power went out from Him and healed them all. (Luke 6:17–19)

The miracles of Jesus can be divided into five distinct categories. According to the gospel records, Jesus had the power to manipulate natural laws, replicate items, cast demons from people, heal all manner of diseases instantly, and raise the dead. As Nicodemus, one of the ruling Pharisees, conceded to Jesus after witnessing some of His miracles:

> Rabbi, we know that You are a teacher come from God;
> for no one can do these signs [miracles] that You do unless
> God is with him. (John 3:2)

Frequently, Jesus Himself would point to His ability to perform miracles (or *works* as He often called them) as proof of His deity:

For the works which the Father has given Me to finish—
the very works that I do—bear witness of Me, that the
Father has sent Me. (John 5:36)

Water into Wine

Jesus' very first public miracle involved the manipulation of matter and
took place at a wedding attended by His mother and some of His disciples.
When the host suddenly realized he had run out of wine, Mary asked
her Son to help out. Jesus obliged and instructed the wedding servers to
gather six water pots capable of holding twenty to thirty gallons each:

> Jesus said to them, "Fill the waterpots with water." And they
> filled them up to the brim. And He said to them, "Draw
> some out now, and take it to the master of the feast." And
> they took it. When the master of the feast had tasted the
> water that was made wine, and did not know where it came
> from (but the servants who had drawn the water knew), the
> master of the feast called the bridegroom. And he said to
> him, "Every man at the beginning sets out the good wine,
> and when the guests have well drunk, then the inferior. You
> have kept the good wine until now!" This beginning of signs
> Jesus did in Cana of Galilee, and manifested His glory; and
> His disciples believed in Him. (John 2:7–11)

The miracle of changing water into wine in Cana set the stage for the
plethora of miracles to come. From there on out, the purpose of every

miracle was twofold: to demonstrate Jesus' compassion for others by solving a personal problem, and to convince those around Him of His deity.

Don't Rock the Boat

As great as the miracle involving the changing of water into wine, it seems overshadowed somewhat in comparison by what would happen on the sea in the days that followed …

> Now when He got into a boat, His disciples followed Him. And suddenly a great tempest arose on the sea, so that the boat was covered with the waves. But He was asleep. Then His disciples came to Him and awoke Him, saying, "Lord, save us! We are perishing!" But He said to them, "Why are you fearful, O you of little faith?" Then He arose and rebuked the winds and the sea, and there was a great calm. So the men marveled, saying, "Who can this be, that even the winds and the sea obey Him?" (Matthew 8:23–27)

The disciples couldn't believe their eyes. This man could control the weather! Even today, sudden, violent storms can arise on the Sea of Galilee without warning. The reaction of these seasoned fishermen to Jesus' abilities was to be expected, for no mere human can command the wind and the waves. And if that weren't enough, another occasion soon arose whereby the disciples found themselves at the mercy of a treacherous sea once again. Only this time, Jesus remained behind on land … at least temporarily:

Immediately Jesus made His disciples get into the boat and go before Him to the other side, while He sent the multitudes away. And when He had sent the multitudes away, He went up on the mountain by Himself to pray. Now when evening came, He was alone there. But the boat was now in the middle of the sea, tossed by the waves, for the wind was contrary. Now in the fourth watch of the night Jesus went to them, walking on the sea. And when the disciples saw Him walking on the sea, they were troubled, saying, "It is a ghost!" And they cried out for fear. But immediately Jesus spoke to them, saying, "Be of good cheer! It is I; do not be afraid." (Matthew 14:22–27)

All You Can Eat

On two occasions, Jesus demonstrated that He could feed a multitude of people by supernaturally multiplying a small amount of fish and bread. The first time He miraculously fed five thousand men and their families until they were all full with only two fish and five loaves of bread. Aside from the resurrection itself, this is the only miracle reported in all four of the gospels, thereby underscoring its significance to the gospel writers:[1]

And they said to Him, "We have here only five loaves and two fish." He said, "Bring them here to Me." Then He commanded the multitudes to sit down on the grass. And He took the five loaves and the two fish, and looking up to heaven, He blessed and broke and gave the loaves to the disciples; and the disciples gave to the multitudes. So they all ate and were filled, and they took up twelve baskets full of the fragments that remained. Now those who had eaten were about five thousand men, besides women and children. (Matthew 14:17–21)

On the second occasion, Jesus fed four thousand men and their families in a similar manner.[2] In the entire history of the world, this type of miracle has never been performed, let alone in front of so many eyewitnesses.

The Insanity Plea

Demon possession has plagued mankind from the beginning of time. Certain cultures have been more susceptible to demonic activity than others, yet no one area of the world has remained immune. No other subject has elicited so many different opinions and generated so much derision, controversy, and confusion.

Judeo-Christian theology classifies demons as fallen angels, which are those angelic beings who, at a certain point in the distant past, collectively rebelled against God and were subsequently cast out of heaven.[3] Generally unseen, these beings are deceiving spirits whose goal is to wreak havoc upon the human race by planting lies in people's minds, among other harmful activities. If given the opportunity, a demon can take up residency within a human host.

People who have become fully demon possessed may seem perfectly normal one minute and violently self-destructive the next. They may suddenly scream out, speak in a strange voice or foreign accent, shout

obscenities or blasphemies, or even lose control of their body in an epi-
leptic-type outburst. Frequently such persons will awaken from an episode
with no recollection of the event.[4] Although demonic spirits may seem
intimidating on the surface, they cower when confronted with the power
of the name of Jesus Christ.

It's not clear what actually triggers demonic possession, although
certain types of behavior such as rebellion against God, eastern religious
meditative practices, occultism, witchcraft, satanism, or certain types of
drug use can open up a person to its possibility. The Greek word translated
as *witchcraft* in the Bible is *pharmakia* from which we derive the word
pharmacy or drugstore. From a biblical perspective, witchcraft and drug
use are synonymous—which is a sobering thought considering the level of
drug abuse (both legal and illegal) in our culture today.[5]

It has become increasingly fashionable to relegate the idea of demon
possession to the world of myth in our modern culture. The twentieth century brought with it the reclassification of psychiatry as a hard science and
the labeling of mental disorders as diseases. Dementia, schizophrenia, and
multiple personalities have become the new definitions of those sometimes
exhibiting the age-old symptoms of demon possession. Many people suffering from such disorders are now routinely given mind-altering medication,
which can occasionally backfire and intensify the problem.

During the time Jesus was on the earth, demon possession in that area
of the Middle East was quite common. His first encounter with a demon-
possessed man occurred in a synagogue in the city of Capernaum. Notice
in this passage how the demon knew exactly who Jesus was:

> Now there was a man in their synagogue with an unclean
> spirit. And he cried out, saying, "Let us alone! What have
> we to do with You, Jesus of Nazareth? Did You come to
> destroy us? I know who You are—the Holy One of God!"

But Jesus rebuked him, saying, "Be quiet, and come out of him!" And when the unclean spirit had convulsed him and cried out with a loud voice, he came out of him. Then they were all amazed, so that they questioned among themselves, saying, "What is this? What new doctrine is this? For with authority He commands even the unclean spirits, and they obey Him." And immediately His fame spread throughout all the region around Galilee. (Mark 1:23–28)

As Jesus' fame grew, many would bring demonically possessed people to Him to heal, and He would. The religious leaders, however, refused to believe that the power being demonstrated by Jesus was from God:

As they went out, behold, they brought to Him a man, mute and demon-possessed. And when the demon was cast out, the mute spoke. And the multitudes marveled, saying, "It was never seen like this in Israel!" But the Pharisees said, "He casts out demons by the ruler of the demons." (Matthew 9:32–34)

Notice that these religious leaders did not deny that Jesus had the power to perform miracles. Nor did they deny that the source of the power was supernatural. Their mistake was that they ascribed it to the wrong source!

A Healing Touch

Perhaps the miracles for which Jesus was most known were His acts of healing diseases. Jesus' compassion and ability to heal broken bodies caused the multitudes to seek Him out. Many rightly believed that the long-awaited Messiah was in their midst.

> Now a leper came to Him, imploring Him, kneeling down to Him and saying to Him, "If You are willing, You can make me clean." Then Jesus, moved with compassion, stretched out His hand and touched him, and said to him, "I am willing; be cleansed." As soon as He had spoken, immediately the leprosy left him, and he was cleansed. (Mark 1:40–42)

The manner in which Jesus carried out the healings differed from case to case. Sometimes Jesus would touch a person. Other times He would simply utter a word. Occasionally, those being healed weren't even in His presence, as was the case with the centurion's servant:

> Now when Jesus had entered Capernaum, a centurion came to Him, pleading with Him, saying, "Lord, my servant is lying at home paralyzed, dreadfully tormented." And Jesus said to him, "I will come and heal him." The centurion answered and said, "Lord, I am not worthy that You should come under my roof. But only speak a word, and my servant will be healed. For I also am a man under authority, having soldiers under me. And I say to this one, 'Go,' and he goes; and to another, 'Come,' and he comes; and to my servant, 'Do this,' and he does it." When Jesus heard it, He marveled, and said to those who followed, "Assuredly, I say to you, I have not found such great faith, not even in Israel!" … Then Jesus said to the centurion, "Go your way; and as you have believed, so

let it be done for you." And his servant was healed that same hour. (Matthew 8:5–10, 13)

Rather than praising God for the miracles swirling around the region, the religious leaders were livid. Jesus had healed a number of people on the Sabbath, which greatly offended the Pharisees, who were more interested in keeping their rules than seeing people made well. As a result, these men began to conspire against Jesus:

> And behold, there was a woman who had a spirit of infirmity eighteen years, and was bent over and could in no way raise herself up. But when Jesus saw her, He called her to Him and said to her, "Woman, you are loosed from your infirmity." And He laid His hands on her, and immediately she was made straight, and glorified God. But the ruler of the synagogue answered with indignation, because Jesus had healed on the Sabbath. (Luke 13:11–14)

Let There Be Light

Isaiah prophesied on at least four occasions that the Messiah would have the power to restore sight.[6] In fact, there are more instances recorded in the New Testament of Jesus performing this miracle than any other.

> When Jesus departed from there, two blind men followed Him, crying out and saying, "Son of David, have

mercy on us!" And when He had come into the house, the blind men came to Him. And Jesus said to them, "Do you believe that I am able to do this?" They said to Him, "Yes, Lord." Then He touched their eyes, saying, "According to your faith let it be to you." And their eyes were opened. (Matthew 9:27–30)

The most unique miracle performed by Jesus is recorded in the eighth chapter of the book of Mark. It concerns the healing of a blind man in the city of Bethsaida. Why is it unique? It is the only example of Jesus healing a person in two stages. On the surface it would appear that the first attempt to heal the man didn't completely work. But upon closer examination, it's clear that a very important medical truth was being revealed:

Then He came to Bethsaida; and they brought a blind man to Him, and begged Him to touch him. So He took the blind man by the hand and led him out of the town. And when He had spit on his eyes and put His hands on him, He asked him if he saw anything. And he looked up and said, "I see men like trees, walking." Then He put His hands on his eyes again and made him look up. And he was restored and saw everyone clearly. (Mark 8:22–25)

Jesus could have just as easily healed the man in one step. But He deliberately did it in two. Why? Because Jesus healed two separate conditions—blindness, and another medical condition that wouldn't even be understood until the twentieth century, known as agnosia.

A man named Virgil had been blind since early childhood and received a lens implant at the age of fifty in 1991. Although the operation success and his vision was restored, the light, movement, and color he saw was meaningless to him. His brain couldn't process it. This is the condition known as agnosia. Virgil even stated at one point that when he looked at a tree, it just didn't make any sense to him. It took a tremendous amount of time before his brain could learn to process the information sent to it by his newly restored optic nerves. This is something people with normal vision do automatically during their first year of life. Virgil's story, incidentally, became the basis for the 1999 film *At First Sight* featuring Val Kilmer.[7]

In the first step of His miracle, Jesus restored the man's sight; in step two He instantly healed the man's brain so he could process the new information. Gospel writer Mark could not have known about agnosia nineteen hundred years before its discovery. The only people who could possibly benefit from the manner in which this passage is written are today's readers, who are aware of this particular medical condition.[8]

Men who appear as walking trees is not just a poetic description; it's a confirmation of medical authenticity, discernable only by the modern-day reader. There is no possible way this passage of Scripture could be considered symbolic or fabricated. What we have here is irrefutable evidence that this miracle did indeed occur.

As the number of astonishing miracles continued to grow, so too did the efforts of the religious leaders to try to quash them. Unfazed, Jesus labored on with His miraculous works. One occasion saw Him heal a man in a most unusual manner:

> He spat on the ground and made clay with the saliva; and He anointed the eyes of the blind man with the clay. And He said to him, "Go, wash in the pool of Siloam" (which is translated, Sent). So he went and washed, and came back seeing. (John 9:6–7)

Was the creation of clay from dirt and saliva just some bizarre ritual, or did Jesus have a purpose for healing the man using this method? Since the man had been born blind, is it possible he didn't actually have eyes? Did Jesus create a pair for him out of the dust of the earth, in the same way God created Adam out of dust? We can't say for sure. What we can say is that this miracle caused a furor among the religious leaders:

> Then the Pharisees also asked him again how he had received his sight. He said to them, "He put clay on my eyes, and I washed, and I see." Therefore some of the Pharisees said, "This Man is not from God, because He does not keep the Sabbath." Others said, "How can a man who is a sinner do such signs?" And there was a division among them. (John 9:15–16)

The man who had been healed became frustrated trying to explain what had happened to him to the religious leaders who were mercilessly grilling him, hoping he would change his story. They simply didn't want to hear the truth. Finally, the man just blurted out the obvious:

> Since the world began it has been unheard of that anyone opened the eyes of one who was born blind. If this Man were not from God, He could do nothing. (John 9:32–33)

Cancel the Funeral

By far, the most dramatic series of miracles Jesus performed concerned His ability to raise people from the dead. Despite great strides in the field of medicine, no one has ever been able to cancel a funeral ... except Jesus:

> And when He came near the gate of the city, behold, a dead man was being carried out, the only son of his mother; and she was a widow. And a large crowd from the city was with her. When the Lord saw her, He had compassion on her and said to her, "Do not weep." Then He came and touched the open coffin, and those who carried him stood still. And He said, "Young man, I say to you, arise." So he who was dead sat up and began to speak. And He presented him to his mother. Then fear came upon all, and they glorified God, saying, "A great prophet has risen up among us"; and, "God has visited His people." And this report about Him went throughout all Judea and all the surrounding region. (Luke 7:12–17)

Sometime later, Jesus met up with a man named Jairus, leader of the synagogue, whose daughter had just died:

> Behold, a ruler came and worshiped Him, saying, "My daughter has just died, but come and lay Your hand on her and she will live." So Jesus arose and followed him, and so did His disciples.... When Jesus came into the ruler's house, and saw the flute players and the noisy crowd wailing, He said to them, "Make room, for the girl is not dead, but sleeping." And they ridiculed Him. But when the crowd was put outside, He went in and took her by the hand, and the girl arose. And the report of this went out into all that land. (Matthew 9:18–19; 23–26)

His most powerful miracle of all was the raising of His friend Lazarus from the dead. Jesus was aware that Lazarus had died but nevertheless took His time arriving at the place of the tomb. In fact, by the time Jesus got there, Lazarus had already been dead and buried in a cave for four days. Lazarus's sisters, Mary and Martha, both believed Jesus had arrived too late to do anything:

> Jesus said, "Take away the stone." Martha, the sister of him who was dead, said to Him, "Lord, by this time there is a stench, for he has been dead four days." Jesus said to her, "Did I not say to you that if you would believe you would see the glory of God?" Then they took away the stone from the place where the dead man was lying. And Jesus lifted up His eyes and said, "Father, I thank You that You have heard Me. And I know that You always hear Me, but because of the people who are standing by I said this, that they may believe that You sent Me." Now when He had said these things, He cried with a loud voice, "Lazarus, come forth!" And he who had died came out bound hand and foot with graveclothes, and his face was wrapped with a cloth. Jesus said to them, "Loose him, and let him go." (John 11:39–44)

For the religious leaders, the raising of Lazarus from the dead was the last straw. The Pharisees had had enough. From this point on they plotted to kill Jesus. It's interesting to see how two different groups of people could look at the same event and have two opposing reactions. While many of those who witnessed this astonishing miracle believed in Jesus, others wanted Him dead. In many ways, it's the same reaction Jesus gets today. Some believe Him, others reject Him. Some love Him, others despise Him.

It should be noted that Jesus' enemies never denied that He had performed these miracles. Many had seen them with their own eyes. Even today, two thousand years later, the evidence of these miracles having actually occurred remains overwhelming.

Running with Scissors

Through the ages, some have felt uncomfortable with the idea of miracles. David Hume was an eighteenth-century Scottish philosopher who was one of the first of the modern era to develop a purely *naturalistic* philosophy.[9] His opposition to miracles was shared by others, including Thomas Jefferson, the third president of the United States. Jefferson was so convinced that the miracles of Jesus were nothing but myth that he actually removed them and other supernatural references from his personal copy of the Bible with a pair of scissors![10] His redacted version was later published as *The Jefferson Bible,* which ultimately failed to find an audience.

The Jesus Seminar is a group of about one to two hundred liberal scholars who gather together twice a year for the sole purpose of criticizing the New Testament. Founded in 1985 by Robert Funk and John Crossan, the group has received a tremendous amount of promotion from all of the major television networks[11] along with major news publications such as *Time, Newsweek*, and *U.S. News & World Report,* which in recent years have regularly utilized the group as part of their various antibiblical campaigns.

The seminar believes that the majority of the New Testament is inaccurate. How did they arrive at such a conclusion? Did they examine any evidence? Did they visit any archeological sites? No ... *they simply voted on whether they believed a certain passage of Scripture was true or not.* They started with the premise that the virgin birth, the deity of Christ, Jesus' atonement for sins, and His resurrection were all false—and concluded that any Scriptures that supported these concepts must also be inaccurate.[12]

The group's first publication, 1993's *The Five Gospels: The Search for the Authentic Words of Jesus*, elevated the Gnostic Gospel of Thomas, a so-called "lost" gospel, above the four gospels contained in the Bible[13] (see chapter 8 for more information). By 1998, the group had dismissed nearly every major event that had been documented in the New Testament, as evidenced by their second publication, *The Acts of Jesus: The Search for the Authentic Deeds of Jesus*. According to this book, Jesus never changed water into wine, walked on water, fed the multitudes, or raised Lazarus from the dead.[14] Additionally, those in the group believed Jesus never actually healed anyone—since the afflictions of every person mentioned in the Scriptures were all "psychosomatic."

Metaphorically Speaking

According to Gnostics, atheists, liberal theologians, and skeptics, the miracles of Jesus are believed to be largely allegorical in nature. His works, as recorded in the Scriptures, are assumed to be purely fictitious and are viewed as teaching devices rather than actual events. Under this presupposition, healing the blind becomes a metaphor for opening one's self up to the truth, healing the paralytic becomes a method of rectifying inaction; healing leprosy symbolizes the removal of social stigmatism, and so forth.

Today, those who are obsessed with trying to strip Jesus of any claim to deity ultimately find themselves waging war not only against the Bible and its documented miracles, but against God Himself. As the Creator of the natural laws that govern the universe, God is not logically constrained by those laws and is therefore able to act outside of them if He so chooses. Simply stating that one *does not believe* in supernatural miracles doesn't prove anything. One would have to prove there is no God in order to claim that miracles are impossible. And so far, no one has ever been able to do that!

Chapter Five

THE GREATEST PROPHET

Moses stands as one of the preeminent heroes of the Judeo-Christian tradition. Jews especially revere him as the greatest of all of Israel's leaders. Not only was Moses a prophet of the highest order, he was also a teacher and a lawgiver who was able to save his people from those who tried to destroy and enslave them. No other prophet of Israel possessed Moses' unique combination of personal attributes.

In chapter 3, we examined many of the Old Testament prophecies that described the various characteristics of the coming Messiah. We also detailed how Jesus of Nazareth fulfilled every one of them. One of the most important messianic prophecies was given by Moses and recorded in the book of Deuteronomy:

> The LORD your God will raise up for you a Prophet like
> me from your midst, from your brethren. Him you shall
> hear, according to all you desired of the LORD your God
> in Horeb in the day of the assembly, saying, "Let me not
> hear again the voice of the LORD my God, nor let me see

this great fire anymore, lest I die." And the LORD said to me: "What they have spoken is good. I will raise up for them a Prophet like you from among their brethren, and will put My words in His mouth, and He shall speak to them all that I command Him." (Deuteronomy 18:15–18)

Uncanny Parallels

Moses' prophecy gave a very clear indication of how the coming Messiah would be identified. Moses' declaration that God would raise up a "Prophet like me" gave the Jews a blueprint for the kind of traits that they should be on the lookout for. Even the Talmud suggested that *the Messiah must be the greatest of future prophets, as being nearest in spirit to our master Moses.*[1]

Just how closely did Jesus' life parallel that of Moses? An investigation of both men's lives reveals that they shared more than fifty similar characteristics. Here are just a few examples …

1. Both men spent their infant years in Egypt, sheltered from those who wished to kill them.
2. Both men grew to become tremendous leaders, teachers, and prophets.
3. Both men fasted for forty days.
4. Both men delivered the law from a mountain—Moses from Mount Sinai, Jesus during the Sermon on the Mount.
5. Both men performed remarkable miracles before eyewitnesses.
6. Both men had power over demonic forces.

7. Both men had power to control bodies of water—Moses parted the Red Sea, Jesus calmed the Sea of Galilee.

8. Both men's faces shone with the glory of heaven—Moses on Mount Sinai, Jesus on the Mount of Transfiguration.

9. As Moses lifted up the brazen serpent to heal his people, Jesus was lifted up on a cross to heal believers from sin.

10. On the seventeenth day of the month of Nisan, Moses offered salvation to the children of Israel by leading them through the Red Sea. Fifteen hundred years later on the same day, Jesus offered salvation to the world by rising from the dead.

11. Both men died on a hill.

12. Neither of their bodies remained in a tomb.[2]

For centuries following Moses' celebrated prophecy, the Jews waited patiently for the appearance of *the Prophet*. Many great prophets of God came and went during this period including David, Isaiah, Jeremiah, Ezekiel, and Daniel, but none had the required attributes of the Messiah.

Nearly fifteen hundred years passed before a man came to the banks of the Jordan River and began baptizing those who wished to be cleansed of their sins.[3] Great crowds congregated around him. Could this be *the Prophet* that had been promised by Moses? The Pharisees sent a group of priests and Levites from Jerusalem to Bethabara to inquire of this man's identity. The man turned out to be John the Baptist:

> And they asked him, "What then? Are you Elijah?" He said, "I am not." "Are you the Prophet?" And he answered, "No." Then they said to him, "Who are you, that we may give an answer to those who sent us? What do you say about yourself?" He said: "I am 'The voice of one crying

in the wilderness: Make straight the way of the LORD,' as
the prophet Isaiah said." (John 1:21–23)

The following day, Jesus Himself arrived on the banks of the Jordan
River and asked John to baptize Him. John immediately announced to
the crowd that this was indeed the Son of God, *the Prophet* who was the
long-awaited fulfillment of Moses' prophecy:[4]

> And John bore witness, saying, "I saw the Spirit descend-
> ing from heaven like a dove, and He remained upon
> Him. I did not know Him, but He who sent me to
> baptize with water said to me, 'Upon whom you see the
> Spirit descending, and remaining on Him, this is He
> who baptizes with the Holy Spirit.' And I have seen and
> testified that this is the Son of God." (John 1:32–34)

Soon, many others in similar fashion began to recognize Jesus of
Nazareth as the promised Prophet:

> Then those men, when they had seen the sign that Jesus
> did, said, "This is truly the Prophet who is to come into
> the world." (John 6:14)

Jesus the Prophet

In the Old Testament, Jesus Christ is the *subject* of prophecies. But in
the New, He becomes the *source* of prophecies. Jesus prophesied more
than any other individual in the Bible. Of the more than 140 prophecies

of His recorded in the New Testament, half were fulfilled during His lifetime or shortly thereafter. The remaining yet-to-be-fulfilled long-term prophecies provide today's readers with a fascinating glimpse into the future by revealing key information about the *last days* and beyond. Many of these prophecies are incredibly specific in their details.

As with the miracles He performed, the short-term prophecies of Jesus helped to solidify His claim of deity in the minds of witnesses who saw these predictions fulfilled before their eyes.

Jesus predicts the centurion's servant will be healed.

The Prophecy:

Now when Jesus had entered Capernaum, a centurion came to Him, pleading with Him, saying, "Lord, my servant is lying at home paralyzed, dreadfully tormented." And Jesus said to him, "I will come and heal him." (Matthew 8:5–7)

The Fulfillment:

Then Jesus said to the centurion, "Go your way; and as you have believed, so let it be done for you." And his servant was healed that same hour. (Matthew 8:13)

Jesus predicts Lazarus will be raised from the dead.

The Prophecy:

Now Martha said to Jesus, "Lord, if You had been here, my brother would not have died. But even now I know that whatever You ask of God, God will give You." Jesus said to her, "Your brother will rise again." (John 11:21–23)

The Fulfillment:

Then they took away the stone from the place where the dead man was lying.... And he who had died came out bound hand and foot with graveclothes, and his face was wrapped with a cloth. Jesus said to them, "Loose him, and let him go." Then many of the Jews who had come to Mary, and had seen the things Jesus did, believed in Him. (John 11:41, 44–45)

Jesus predicts His disciples will find a colt tied up.

The Prophecy:

Go into the village opposite you, where as you enter you will find a colt tied, on which no one has ever sat.

Loose it and bring it here. And if anyone asks you, "Why are you loosing it?" thus you shall say to him, "Because the Lord has need of it." (Luke 19:30–31)

The Fulfillment:

So those who were sent went their way and found it just as He had said to them. (Luke 19:32)

Jesus predicts His disciples will find a room prepared for the Passover.

The Prophecy:

And He sent out two of His disciples and said to them, "Go into the city, and a man will meet you carrying a pitcher of water; follow him. Wherever he goes in, say to the master of the house, 'The Teacher says, "Where is the guest room in which I may eat the Passover with My disciples?"' Then he will show you a large upper room, furnished and prepared; there make ready for us." (Mark 14:13–15)

The Fulfillment:

So His disciples went out, and came into the city, and found it just as He had said to them. (Mark 14:16)

Jesus predicts Judas will betray Him.

The Prophecy:

Now as they were eating, He said, "Assuredly, I say to you, one of you will betray Me." And they were exceedingly sorrowful, and each of them began to say to Him, "Lord, is it I?" He answered and said, "He who dipped his hand with Me in the dish will betray Me. The Son of Man indeed goes just as it is written of Him, but woe to that man by whom the Son of Man is betrayed! It would have been good for that man if he had not been born." Then Judas, who was betraying Him, answered and said, "Rabbi, is it I?" He said to him, "You have said it." (Matthew 26:21–25)

The Fulfillment:

And while He was still speaking, behold, Judas, one of the twelve, with a great multitude with swords and clubs, came from the chief priests and elders of the people. Now His betrayer had given them a sign, saying, "Whomever I kiss, He is the One; seize Him." Immediately he went up to Jesus and said, "Greetings, Rabbi!" and kissed Him. (Matthew 26:47–49)

Jesus predicts His disciples will flee following His arrest.

The Prophecy:

Then Jesus said to them, "All of you will be made to stumble because of Me this night, for it is written: 'I will strike the Shepherd, and the sheep of the flock will be scattered.'" (Matthew 26:31)

The Fulfillment:

Then all the disciples forsook Him and fled. And those who had laid hold of Jesus led Him away to Caiaphas the high priest, where the scribes and the elders were assembled. (Matthew 26:56–57)

Jesus predicts Peter will deny Him three times.

The Prophecy:

Jesus said to him, "Assuredly, I say to you that this night, before the rooster crows, you will deny Me three times." Peter said to Him, "Even if I have to die with You, I will not deny You!" (Matthew 26:34–35)

The Fulfillment:

Now Peter sat outside in the courtyard. And a servant girl
came to him, saying, "You also were with Jesus of Galilee."
But he denied it before them all, saying, "I do not know
what you are saying." And when he had gone out to the
gateway, another girl saw him and said to those who were
there, "This fellow also was with Jesus of Nazareth." But
again he denied with an oath, "I do not know the Man!"
And a little later those who stood by came up and said to
Peter, "Surely you also are one of them, for your speech
betrays you." Then he began to curse and swear, saying,
"I do not know the Man!" Immediately a rooster crowed.
And Peter remembered the word of Jesus who had said
to him, "Before the rooster crows, you will deny Me
three times." So he went out and wept bitterly. (Matthew
26:69–75)

Most of Christ's short-term prophecies revolve around His impending death, burial, and resurrection. On numerous occasions, Jesus
attempted to prepare His disciples for the inevitability of these events.
However, more often than not, the disciples were confused and troubled
by such talk; for they, like many of the Jews of that time, expected
Jesus to immediately assume control of the government. But fulfilling
His role as heir to David's throne would have to wait until His second
coming. Becoming a substitute for our sins and conquering death had
to come first ...

Jesus predicts He will be crucified and rise again the third day.

The Prophecy:

Now Jesus, going up to Jerusalem, took the twelve disciples aside on the road and said to them, "Behold, we are going up to Jerusalem, and the Son of Man will be betrayed to the chief priests and to the scribes; and they will condemn Him to death, and deliver Him to the Gentiles to mock and to scourge and to crucify. And the third day He will rise again." (Matthew 20:17–19)

The Fulfillment:

Do not be alarmed. You seek Jesus of Nazareth, who was crucified. He is risen! He is not here. See the place where they laid Him. (Mark 16:6)

More Unfolding Prophecies

Jesus made a number of predictions that came to fruition shortly after His resurrection, while others were fulfilled during the succeeding centuries ...

*Jesus predicts He will see His disciples in Galilee
after His resurrection.*

The Prophecy:

"But after I have been raised, I will go before you to
Galilee." (Mark 14:28)

The Fulfillment:

Then the eleven disciples went away into Galilee, to the
mountain which Jesus had appointed for them. When
they saw Him, they worshiped Him; but some doubted.
(Matthew 28:16–17)

*Jesus predicts the Holy Spirit will fill His
disciples.*

The Prophecy:

But the Helper, the Holy Spirit, whom the Father will
send in My name, He will teach you all things, and bring
to your remembrance all things that I said to you. (John
14:26)

The Fulfillment:

When the Day of Pentecost had fully come, they were all with one accord in one place. And suddenly there came a sound from heaven, as of a rushing mighty wind, and it filled the whole house where they were sitting. Then there appeared to them divided tongues, as of fire, and one sat upon each of them. And they were all filled with the Holy Spirit and began to speak with other tongues, as the Spirit gave them utterance. (Acts 2:1–4)

Jesus predicts Jerusalem's temple will be destroyed.

The Prophecy:

Then Jesus went out and departed from the temple, and His disciples came up to show Him the buildings of the temple. And Jesus said to them, "Do you not see all these things? Assuredly, I say to you, not one stone shall be left here upon another, that shall not be thrown down." (Matthew 24:1–2)

The Fulfillment:

In the year AD 70, Rome's army, led by its soon-to-be emperor Titus, conquered the city of Jerusalem. The city, along with the Jewish temple, which had been refurbished by King Herod only a few decades earlier, was destroyed with no stone left on top of another, just as Jesus had predicted. Famed Jewish-Roman historian Josephus was an actual eyewitness to the destruction and documented the city's demise.[5] It is estimated that more than a million people were killed during the siege—the majority of whom were Jewish. Another 97,000 were captured and enslaved.[6] Many Christians who were aware of the prophecy had already left the city four years earlier and were spared the massacre as a result.[7] Today, the Wailing Wall in Jerusalem serves as a reminder of this prophecy—the stone blocks that make up the wall come from the temple, which, to this day, has not been rebuilt.

Jesus predicts His church will survive.

The Prophecy:

I will build My church, and the gates of Hades shall not prevail against it. (Matthew 16:18)

The Fulfillment:

In the two thousand years since that prediction was given, the church, which is made up of those around the world who believe in Jesus Christ, despite unparalleled persecution throughout history, has remained strong and continues to grow.[8]

What Lies Ahead

The other half of Jesus' prophecies (those yet to be fulfilled) deal primarily with the *end times*. Many of these future events are literally earth-shattering in their scope and are reinforced by other biblical prophets from both the Old and New Testaments. The *last days* scenario includes the following events occurring in this order:

1. *The Rapture of the Church*—Believers will be instantly taken from earth to heaven (John 14:2–3; 1 Corinthians 15:51–57; 1 Thessalonians 4:13–18).

2. *The Judgment Seat of Christ*—Believers will be rewarded for their good works (1 Corinthians 3:11–15; 2 Corinthians 5:9–11).

3. *The Tribulation*—A seven-year period of unprecedented death and destruction will be experienced by those left behind on earth (Matthew 24:3–28; Mark 13:3–23; Luke 21:7–24; Revelation 6:1—19:21).

4. *The Second Coming of Christ*—Jesus will return to earth at the conclusion of the tribulation (Matthew 24:29–31; Mark 13:24–27; Luke 21:25–28).

5. *The Millennial Kingdom*—A one-thousand-year period of peace on earth will be ruled over by Christ Himself (Matthew 25:31–40; Revelation 20:1–6)

6. *The Great White Throne Judgment/The Eternal Realm*—Believers will remain with Christ while nonbelievers are judged and cast into hell. (Matthew 25:41–46; Revelation 20:11—22:5).

The seven-year period referred to as the tribulation will be controlled by a charismatic and deceitful world leader known as the Antichrist. He will require that every human being on the face of the earth take a *mark* on their hand or forehead, which is the only means anyone will be able to buy or sell. This mark will be designated by the number 666.[9] Those who take the mark will do so in rebellion against God and will forever forfeit a place in heaven.[10] Millions will be put to death for refusing to take the mark.[11] This world leader will also instigate the battle of Armageddon, the greatest war ever to be fought. Three-fourths of the world's population will be killed during this time.[12] It's no wonder Jesus used the following words to describe this awesome period:

> For then there will be great tribulation, such as has not
> been since the beginning of the world until this time, no,
> nor ever shall be. And unless those days were shortened,
> no flesh would be saved; but for the elect's sake those days
> will be shortened. (Matthew 24:21–22)

The *last days* prophecies of Christ were revealed primarily on two different occasions. The first was before an audience of Jesus' disciples on the Mount of Olives in Jerusalem. This is referred to as the Olivet Discourse.[13] It is recorded by three of the four gospel writers in the pages of Matthew, Mark, and Luke, but curiously not by John. The apostle John was instead chosen to be the recipient of a larger series of prophecies that formed the basis of the book of Revelation, which provided even more specific details about the *last days*.

Jesus predicts the rapture will occur at a time when it's least expected.

> But of that day and hour no one knows, not even the angels of heaven, but My Father only. But as the days of Noah were, so also will the coming of the Son of Man be. For as in the days before the flood, they were eating and drinking, marrying and giving in marriage, until the day that Noah entered the ark, and did not know until the flood came and took them all away, so also will the coming of the Son of Man be. Then two men will be in the field: one will be taken and the other left. Two women will be grinding at the mill: one will be taken and the other left. Watch therefore, for you do not know what hour your Lord is coming. (Matthew 24:36–42)

Jesus predicts (raptured) believers will be kept from the tribulation.

> Because you have kept My command to persevere, I also will keep you from the hour of trial which shall come upon the whole world, to test those who dwell on the earth. (Revelation 3:10)

Jesus predicts believers will be rewarded for their works.

> And behold, I am coming quickly, and My reward is with

Me, to give to every one according to his work. (Revelation 22:12)

Jesus predicts various signs will precede the tribulation.

For nation will rise against nation, and kingdom against kingdom. And there will be famines, pestilences, and earthquakes in various places. All these are the beginning of sorrows. (Matthew 24:7–8)

Jesus predicts believers will be martyred during the tribulation.

Then they will deliver you up to tribulation and kill you, and you will be hated by all nations for My name's sake. (Matthew 24:9)

Jesus predicts family members will turn against one another during the tribulation.

Now brother will betray brother to death, and a father his child; and children will rise up against parents and cause them to be put to death. (Mark 13:12)

Jesus predicts spiritual deception, crime, and diminished love will run rampant during the tribulation.

> Then many false prophets will rise up and deceive many. And because lawlessness will abound, the love of many will grow cold. (Matthew 24:11–12)

Jesus predicts the Antichrist will desecrate the temple in Jerusalem at midpoint in the tribulation.

> "Therefore when you see the 'abomination of desolation,' spoken of by Daniel the prophet, standing in the holy place" (whoever reads, let him understand), "then let those who are in Judea flee to the mountains." (Matthew 24:15–16)

Jesus predicts He will return to earth at the conclusion of the tribulation.

> Immediately after the tribulation of those days the sun will be darkened, and the moon will not give its light; the stars will fall from heaven, and the powers of the heavens will be shaken. Then the sign of the Son of Man will appear in heaven, and then all the tribes of the earth will mourn, and they will see the Son of Man coming on the clouds of heaven with power and great glory. (Matthew 24:29–30)

Jesus predicts He will set up His millennial kingdom following His second coming.

> When the Son of Man comes in His glory, and all the holy angels with Him, then He will sit on the throne of His glory. All the nations will be gathered before Him, and He will separate them one from another, as a shepherd divides his sheep from the goats. And He will set the sheep on His right hand, but the goats on the left. Then the King will say to those on His right hand, "Come, you blessed of My Father, inherit the kingdom prepared for you from the foundation of the world." (Matthew 25:31–34)

Jesus predicts He will be able to discern nonbelievers from believers.

> Not everyone who says to Me, "Lord, Lord," shall enter the kingdom of heaven, but he who does the will of My Father in heaven. Many will say to Me in that day, "Lord, Lord, have we not prophesied in Your name, cast out demons in Your name, and done many wonders in Your name?" And then I will declare to them, "I never knew you; depart from Me, you who practice lawlessness!" (Matthew 7:21–23)

Jesus predicts angels will assist Him at the final judgment.

> So it will be at the end of the age. The angels will come
> forth, separate the wicked from among the just, and cast
> them into the furnace of fire. There will be wailing and
> gnashing of teeth. (Matthew 13:49–50)

Jesus predicts there will be a place for believers in heaven.

> Let not your heart be troubled; you believe in God, believe
> also in Me. In My Father's house are many mansions; if it
> were not so, I would have told you. I go to prepare a place
> for you. And if I go and prepare a place for you, I will
> come again and receive you to Myself; that where I am,
> there you may be also. (John 14:1–3)

Again, due to Jesus Christ's 100 percent prophetic accuracy rate, along
with the 100 percent accuracy rate for all other biblical prophets, it's logical
to assume that the prophecies concerning the *last days*—including those
involving the rapture, the rewarding of believers, the tribulation, the second
coming, the millennial kingdom, and the judgment of nonbelievers—will
indeed come to pass in due time just as predicted. When? That's known
only to God. However, many biblical scholars believe it could be very soon
indeed based on the fact that our generation has seen more fulfilled signs
of "the end of the age" than any generation before us.[14]

Chapter Six

EVERYBODY KNOWS HE ROSE

It has been said that the resurrection of Christ is the cornerstone of Christianity ... for without the resurrection there would be no Christianity. It is therefore not surprising that today's Gnostic revivalists and historical reconstructionists are obsessed with trying to argue that it never occurred.

The resurrection of Jesus is mentioned more than one hundred times in the New Testament. The disciples, who were all eyewitnesses to the event, knew firsthand that it was a fact (Acts 2:32). The resurrection subsequently became the foundation for their faith and the primary topic of their preaching. It was the reality of the resurrection that turned a group of depressed and despondent disciples into a radical faction of bold and determined leaders who were prepared to become martyrs if necessary. Had there been one shred of evidence that the resurrection of Christ was a fraud, this transformation would not have occurred. Likewise, the miraculous formation and continued existence of the Christian church during the last two millennia would never have happened were it not for the certainty of the resurrection.

In Search of the Lost Story

> No man has ever written, pro or con, on the subject of
> Christ's Resurrection, without finding himself compelled
> to face this problem of Joseph's empty tomb.[1]

An early example of the Gnostic revival in the modern era took place
in 1965 with the publication of the book *The Passover Plot* by liberal
theologian Hugh Schonfield. In his book, Schonfield portrays Jesus as
a scriptural scholar of sorts who has messianic delusions. He secretly
schemes to "fulfill" all the necessary Old Testament prophecies concerning the Messiah, culminating with his feigned death on the cross and
subsequent *resuscitation* in the tomb. With the conspiratorial help of
Lazarus and Joseph of Arimathea, Schonfield's Jesus hopes to convince
his disciples, who are unaware of the charade in progress, that he is indeed
the Messiah.

According to Schonfield, the scam would have worked if the Roman
soldier hadn't pierced Jesus with his sword while he was on the cross. This
caused Jesus to die. Fortunately for Schonfield, the disciples mistook other
people for Christ in the days following the crucifixion, thus convincing
them that he had indeed risen from the dead. This is Schonfield's amazing
version of the birth of Christianity.[2]

How the delusional and dishonest acts of one man (Schonfield's Jesus)
combined with the naive stupidity of eleven others (Schonfield's disciples)
could result in this Jesus achieving unprecedented worldwide elevation
above every other human on the planet continuously for two thousand
years is truly incredible. In fact, Schonfield's attempt to explain away the
resurrection and its subsequent effect on the world is harder to believe
than the actual historical facts surrounding the resurrection itself!

Both *The Passover Plot* book and subsequent 1976 movie of the same name render Jesus as a cunning, conniving, deceptive imposter,[3] in contrast to the gospel and other historical accounts which clearly depict Him as a man of honesty and integrity. And as we've already discussed, the basic premise that Jesus could somehow force-manipulate the fulfillment of over one hundred Old Testament prophecies is, in a word, impossible.

How was Jesus able to manipulate, for example, the reactions of others with such precision? How did he manage to extract Peter's triple denial, Pilate's sentence of crucifixion, or Judas's betrayal and acquisition of exactly thirty pieces of silver? In fact, anyone possessing the magnitude of manipulative power needed to pull off such a con *would have to be divine*—which is the very conclusion Schonfield was hoping to avoid!

Which brings us back to that pesky piece of evidence involving the heavily guarded empty tomb. How does Schonfield explain that?

> We may dismiss the story in Matthew alone that the chief priests requested Pilate that a guard be set over the tomb, and that they posted a watch.[4]

Why should we "dismiss" the documented account that there was a large group of Roman soldiers guarding the tomb? Because it's an insurmountable obstacle to the stolen-body theory, that's why. This is standard procedure for most modern-day "scholars" wishing to undermine the New Testament's account of the resurrection: Simply ignore whatever evidence is necessary to conform to a preconceived bias, and offer no proof or reason for doing so.

The cover of Michael Baigent's best seller *The Jesus Papers* boldly declares to expose "the greatest cover-up in history." And just what is the greatest cover-up in history? That Jesus didn't actually die on the cross …

a claim that serves only to reinforce the wisdom of King Solomon who stated that "there's nothing new under the sun." The key to Baigent's theory is contained in the sponge that is offered to Jesus during the crucifixion:

> The sponge was soaked not in vinegar, a substance that would have revived Jesus, but rather in something that would have caused him to lose consciousness—some sort of drug,… It was known that a sponge soaked in a mixture of opium and other compounds such as belladonna and hashish served as a good anesthetic.… All that remained then was for Jesus to be taken down from the cross, apparently lifeless but in reality unconscious, and taken to a private tomb where medicines could be used to revive him. He would then be whisked away from the scene.[5]

Does Baigent have any *evidence* for this particular drug concoction? Does he have any *evidence* for the medicines used to revive Jesus in the tomb? And why didn't the Roman soldiers guarding the tomb try to stop Jesus from being "whisked away"? To fully understand Michael Baigent's desire to rewrite history, one must take into consideration not only his background in (anti-Christian) mysticism, but his admitted disdain for the Scriptures:

> Certainly the New Testament is bad history. This is impossible to deny. The texts are inconsistent, incomplete, garbled, and biased. It is possible to deconstruct the New Testament to the point where nothing remains but a heavily biased, dogmatic Christian mythology.[6]

Emphatically contradicting Michael Baigent's theory is author James Tabor. In his book *The Jesus Dynasty*, Tabor argues that Jesus most certainly did die on the cross and the body was subsequently removed from the tomb during the night—most likely by his mother, Mary, along with a few other women.[7] (Again, where are the guards? And how did these women manage to move the four-thousand-pound boulder blocking the entrance to the tomb?) With the deceased and unresurrected Jesus now out of the picture, the job of carrying on his work, including the formation of the Christian church, is then handed off to James, the brother of Jesus, according to Tabor:

> Three facts appear to be indisputable: first, that Jesus was truly dead; second, that he was hastily and temporarily buried in an unknown tomb; and third, that the movement Jesus began did not end with his death but revived and found new life under the leadership of Jesus' brother James.[8]

Despite being in direct conflict with one another, Baigent's and Tabor's theories both manage to deny the reality of the resurrection, which is, of course, the primary goal of today's Gnostic revivalists. These recycled arguments are really nothing more than attempts to explain the empty tomb from a *naturalistic* perspective.

The one common denominator in all of these theories is the foundational assumption that the original texts are inaccurate. The overriding supposition is that today's elitist "scholars," who have a built-in bias against Jesus and the precision of the Scriptures, are somehow better equipped to comment on the events of two thousand years ago than the eyewitnesses who were actually there.

Eyewitness Accounts

The resurrection of Jesus Christ is recorded in all four of the gospels—
Matthew 28, Mark 16, Luke 24, and John 20. Each account provides a
different perspective of the events occurring on that resurrection morning. Some critics have jumped on the narrative differences, suggesting
these variations are proof of their unreliability. However, one should be
all the more suspicious if these four accounts written by four different
people in four different places at four different times turned out to be
exactly alike.

A police officer, for example, who is attempting to piece together
the events leading up to a traffic accident would prefer to gather information from four eyewitnesses rather than just one. Despite nominal
differences in testimony, a much clearer and more substantial version of
events can be gleaned, with each eyewitness offering up a unique piece
of the puzzle from his or her individual point of view. The same holds
true for all of the events documented in the four gospels, including the
resurrection.

Combined together, the gospel accounts of the resurrection paint a
detailed picture of victory and hope that ultimately serves to vanquish the
perceived defeat and tragedy of the preceding days. The resurrection acts
as the perfect validation to Christ's sinless life … a life characterized by
wisdom, leadership, and powerful acts of compassion, healing, and sacrifice. In fact, it is the resurrection that makes it possible for everyone on
earth who so chooses to have their sins forgiven, to maintain a relationship
with their Creator, and to receive the assurance of eternal life. Without it,
Christianity is simply a colossal hoax and a waste of time.

Prelude to the Resurrection

Once the crucifixion was complete and Jesus verified as dead by the Roman guards, a council member named Joseph was given charge over the body by Pontius Pilate.

> Joseph of Arimathea, a prominent council member, who was himself waiting for the kingdom of God, coming and taking courage, went in to Pilate and asked for the body of Jesus. Pilate marveled that He was already dead; and summoning the centurion, he asked him if He had been dead for some time. So when he found out from the centurion, he granted the body to Joseph. Then he bought fine linen, took Him down, and wrapped Him in the linen. And he laid Him in a tomb which had been hewn out of the rock, and rolled a stone against the door of the tomb. And Mary Magdalene and Mary the mother of Joses observed where He was laid. (Mark 15:43–47)

No doubt the religious leaders had a difficult time sleeping that night. Maybe their hearts were convicted. Perhaps a few recognized that they had executed an innocent man. Others may have scoured the Scriptures by candlelight, reading and rereading the messianic prophecies while Jesus' own predictions about His impending death and resurrection reverberated in their ears. *Was this the promised Messiah, and would He rise again on the third day?* Indeed, there were some who knew exactly who this man was, and they knew what might happen come Sunday. And they weren't about to take any chances:

> On the next day, which followed the Day of Preparation,

the chief priests and Pharisees gathered together to Pilate, saying, "Sir, we remember, while He was still alive, how that deceiver said, 'After three days I will rise.' Therefore command that the tomb be made secure until the third day, lest His disciples come by night and steal Him away, and say to the people, 'He has risen from the dead.' So the last deception will be worse than the first." Pilate said to them, "You have a guard; go your way, make it as secure as you know how." So they went and made the tomb secure, sealing the stone and setting the guard. (Matthew 27:62–66)

In sealing the tomb and placing the Roman guards on watch, the religious leaders in essence sealed their own fates. They did everything they could to ensure that no one could get in (or out) of the tomb. But the plan backfired ... for nothing could have stopped Jesus from rising on the third day. The chief priests and Pharisees had succeeded only in making it more difficult for themselves. They then had to come up with a plausible explanation for the empty tomb that circumvented the sealed stone and Roman guards:

Now after the Sabbath, as the first day of the week began to dawn, Mary Magdalene and the other Mary came to see the tomb. And behold, there was a great earthquake; for an angel of the Lord descended from heaven, and came and rolled back the stone from the door, and sat on it. His countenance was like lightning, and his clothing as white as snow. And the guards shook for fear of him, and became like dead men. But the angel answered and said to the women, "Do not be afraid, for I know that

you seek Jesus who was crucified. He is not here; for He
is risen, as He said. Come, see the place where the Lord
lay. And go quickly and tell His disciples that He is risen
from the dead, and indeed He is going before you into
Galilee; there you will see Him. Behold, I have told you."
(Matthew 28:1–7)

The religious leaders were bound and determined to keep the truth
hidden. In doing so, they came up with the first *alternate empty tomb
scenario*. It's one that can easily be shown to be fallacious, but that hasn't
stopped it from being endlessly repeated throughout succeeding centuries
by skeptics, atheists, and Gnostics:

Some of the guard came into the city and reported to the
chief priests all the things that had happened. When they
had assembled with the elders and consulted together,
they gave a large sum of money to the soldiers, saying,
"Tell them, 'His disciples came at night and stole Him
away while we slept.' And if this comes to the governor's
ears, we will appease him and make you secure." So
they took the money and did as they were instructed.
(Matthew 28:11–15)

The disciples could not have stolen the body. They had absolutely no
motive to do so. All were in a state of shock and deep depression following
the crucifixion. Nor did they have the opportunity to steal it with the
tomb sealed and the Roman soldiers guarding it. And how would stealing
the body transform these broken and defeated disciples into bold leaders
who were now willing to die for their beliefs? Only the reality of the resurrection could have accomplished that.

The Evidence Mounts

> The resurrection of Jesus Christ is either one of the most wicked, vicious, heartless hoaxes ever foisted on the minds of human beings—or it is the most remarkable fact of history.[9]

The one piece of historical evidence that cannot be denied is the reality of the empty tomb. The women who were first to arrive on the scene found it empty; Peter and John found it empty; the Roman guards who were convinced they would be executed for failing to do their duty fearfully reported it empty; the religious leaders believed it was empty; historians agree it was empty; even today's skeptics reluctantly agree it was empty— hence the endless desperate attempts to come up with a credible-sounding alternative to the resurrection. Listen to the words of one scholar who accepts the empty tomb:

> I claim to be an historian. My approach to Classics is historical. And I tell you that the evidence for the life, the death, and the resurrection of Christ is better authenticated than most of the facts of ancient history.[10]

Had the resurrection been a fraud perpetrated by the disciples, it would have made sense for them to travel to some land far away from where the events took place in order to further their myth. However, they remained in Jerusalem, the very city where the resurrection occurred and the witnesses resided, and began using the empty tomb as the primary piece of evidence in their teaching. As professor Dr. Paul Althaus said:

The resurrection could have not been maintained in
Jerusalem for a single day, for a single hour, if the empti-
ness of the tomb had not been established as a fact for all
concerned.[11]

Following the resurrection of Christ, large numbers of people began
to believe in Jesus as the Messiah. The religious leaders were furious. All
they needed to do to stop the conversions from taking place was to pro-
duce the body of Jesus. But they couldn't. So they began to discuss how
they should go about killing the disciples. Gamaliel, a leading council
member and a reasonable man, tried to get everyone to come to their
senses:

> Then one in the council stood up, a Pharisee named
> Gamaliel, a teacher of the law held in respect by all the
> people.... And he said to them: "Men of Israel, take
> heed to yourselves what you intend to do regarding
> these men.... Keep away from these men and let them
> alone; for if this plan or this work is of men, it will come
> to nothing; but if it is of God, you cannot overthrow
> it—lest you even be found to fight against God." (Acts
> 5:34–35, 38–39)

Infallible Proofs

> He also presented Himself alive after His suffering by
> many infallible proofs, being seen by them during forty

days and speaking of the things pertaining to the kingdom of God. (Acts 1:3)

Eyewitnesses to the postresurrection appearances of Jesus provide
the most compelling evidence of all that He was indeed alive after being
executed on the cross. These "infallible proofs" include His appearance
before more than five hundred people, overwhelming evidence that
would stand up in any court. The New Testament reports ten such
appearances (although there were probably many more) over a period of
forty days beginning on the morning of the resurrection and continuing until His ascension into heaven. Following His resurrection, Jesus
appeared:

1. To Mary Magdalene in the early morning hours of the first day of
   the week. (Mark 16:9–11; John 20:14–18)
2. To a group of women that same morning. (Matthew 28:1–10; Luke
   24:1–7)
3. To the apostle Peter that afternoon. (Luke 24:34; 1 Corinthians
   15:5)
4. To Cleopas and another disciple on the road to Emmaus later in the
   afternoon. (Mark 16:12–13; Luke 24:13–33)
5. To ten of the apostles, excluding Thomas, plus a group of others
   that evening. (Luke 24:36–43; John 20:19–24)
6. To all eleven apostles eight days later. (John 20:26–29)
7. To a group of disciples on the Sea of Galilee. (John 21:4–14)
8. To a group of more than five hundred on a mountain in Galilee.
   (Matthew 28:16–20; 1 Corinthians 15:6)
9. To James under unknown circumstances. (1 Corinthians 15:7)
10. To the apostles prior to the ascension on the Mount of Olives in
    Jerusalem. (Luke 24:50–52; Acts 1:4–8)

One of the greatest confirmations of the validity of the eyewitnesses comes from the pen of the apostle Paul. In writing to the Corinthian church less than thirty years after the events in question, Paul reminds them that the majority of the more than five hundred witnesses who saw the postresurrection Jesus were still alive and could be questioned if necessary:

> For I delivered to you first of all that which I also received: that Christ died for our sins according to the Scriptures, and that He was buried, and that He rose again the third day according to the Scriptures, and that He was seen by Cephas [Peter], then by the twelve. After that He was seen by over five hundred brethren at once, of whom the greater part remain to the present, but some have fallen asleep [died]. (1 Corinthians 15:3–6)

Dr. Edwin Yamauchi, professor of history at Miami University, explains it well:

> What gives a special authority to the list [of witnesses] as historical evidence is the reference to most of the five hundred brethren being still alive. St. Paul says in effect, "If you do not believe me, you can ask them." Such a statement in an admittedly genuine letter written within thirty years of the event is almost as strong evidence as one could hope to get for something that happened nearly two thousand years ago.[12]

It is important to understand that the resurrected Jesus did not come back in some type of spiritual or ghostly body, but in a literal, physical body of flesh and bone. A physically resurrected Christ walked, talked, and ate with His disciples ...

> Now as they said these things, Jesus Himself stood in the midst of them, and said to them, "Peace to you." But they were terrified and frightened, and supposed they had seen a spirit. And He said to them, "Why are you troubled? And why do doubts arise in your hearts? Behold My hands and My feet, that it is I Myself. Handle Me and see, for a spirit does not have flesh and bones as you see I have." When He had said this, He showed them His hands and His feet. But while they still did not believe for joy, and marveled, He said to them, "Have you any food here?" So they gave Him a piece of a broiled fish and some honeycomb. And He took it and ate in their presence. (Luke 24:36–43)

Jesus' resurrected body was physical, but it was also different—it was now an eternal body. Unlike before, He could now pass through walls to get from one place to another. He could be touched, but He was no longer subject to the confines of time and space. However, his new body still bore the scars of His crucifixion, as the apostle Thomas could attest:

> So he [Thomas] said to them, "Unless I see in His hands the print of the nails, and put my finger into the print of the nails, and put my hand into His side, I will not believe." And after eight days His disciples were again inside, and Thomas with them. Jesus came, the doors being shut, and stood in the midst, and said,

"Peace to you!" Then He said to Thomas, "Reach your
finger here, and look at My hands; and reach your hand
here, and put it into My side. Do not be unbelieving,
but believing." And Thomas answered and said to Him,
"My Lord and my God!" (John 20:25–28)

Had it not been for the postresurrection reunion between the disciples
and the living Christ, Christianity would not exist. Those experiences not
only convinced Jesus' followers that He had indeed risen, it transformed
them into dynamic teachers who were now willing to give up their lives in
order to proclaim His message.

Many of them were arrested, imprisoned, and beaten. Eventually all
eleven of the disciples would die a martyr's death, with the exception of
the apostle John. (It is believed John was boiled in oil for testifying that
he had seen the resurrected Christ but somehow managed to survive the
ordeal. He was eventually imprisoned on the Isle of Patmos.) The question
is … would these men have been so willing to suffer and die for a lie?
Would they have been so bold if this whole thing was a charade? Yet none
of them recanted when faced with death. Why? Because they had seen
Him alive. They had spoken with Him. They had touched Him. Professor
Thomas Arnold of Oxford University sums it up:

I know of no one fact in the history of mankind which
is proved by better and fuller evidence of every sort, to
the understanding of a fair inquirer, than the great sign
which God hath given us that Christ died and rose again
from the dead.[13]

Invasion of the Body Snatchers

The enemies of Christ have had two thousand years to come up with a believable alternative to the resurrection story. They have had centuries to formulate, process, and refine their arguments as to what happened to the body of Jesus following the crucifixion. One can only shake one's head in disbelief and ask, "Is this the best you can do?" Remember, the quest to stop the resurrection began *the day before it actually occurred* and has continued to this very day:

> From the very beginning of Christ's work on earth, and throughout the New Testament, the resurrection of Christ was bitterly and continually opposed.... The chief priests and Pharisees ... were, even before Christ rose from the dead, determined that such an event must not occur. They did not want Him to rise from the dead, and they made every possible provision that He shouldn't rise from the dead. This is not the way men act who are seeking the truth.[14]

The Swoon Theory

This theory, held by Michael Baigent and other Gnostics, states that Christ merely passed out while on the cross and was resuscitated shortly thereafter. Remember, Jesus' death was confirmed multiple times, both on the cross and afterward—*by professional executioners*. The most powerful man in the region, Pontius Pilate, required verification of the death before he would release the body to Joseph. Even David Strauss, the famous nineteenth-century skeptic, rules out the swoon theory as a possibility:

It is impossible that one who had just come forth from the grave half dead, who crept about weak and ill, who stood in need of medical treatment, of bandaging, strengthening, and tender care, and who at last succumbed to suffering, could ever have given to the disciples that impression that He was a conqueror over death and the grave—that He was the Prince of Life—which lay at the bottom of their future ministry. Such a resuscitation ... could by no possibility have changed their sorrow into enthusiasm, or elevated their reverence into worship.[15]

Dr. Frank Young, a medical doctor with a PhD in microbiology, was a research specialist at the Scripps Research Center in La Jolla, California, who later became commissioner of the Food and Drug Administration. He told me while he was a member of the church I pastored in San Diego that the swoon theory was a medical impossibility. Jesus had been beaten beyond recognition prior to being placed on the cross, had spikes driven through His hands and feet, had been stabbed in the side with a spear, and had lost tremendous amounts of blood. He was then wrapped tightly with over a hundred pounds of ointments and wrappings and placed in a cold tomb. No one could have survived such treatment. Furthermore, once inside the tomb, how could Jesus, in His weakened condition, dislodge Himself from the great weight of the wrappings, break the Roman seal, push away a four-thousand-pound boulder, overpower the guards, and seek out the disciples?

Sooner or later Jesus would die anyway and thereafter any preaching of the resurrection would cease altogether. Either way, the Christian church would not exist today were it not for the fact of the bodily resurrection of Jesus.

The Wrong-Tomb Theory

This theory supposes that the women went to the wrong tomb on the morning of the resurrection, even though the text clearly shows them at the correct tomb during the burial (Matthew 27:61; Mark 15:47). This theory not only casts the women as morons, it portrays much of the city's populace in an equally bad light for believing that a resurrection had occurred based on such an error. This hypothesis also assumes that the lives of the apostles would dramatically change, and that the Christian church would grow and thrive for the next two thousand years based on *a complete lack of evidence*. You can be sure that had such a mistake been made, the world's most extensive tomb search would have been ordered by the chief priests, who desperately needed the body as proof that there was no resurrection. Of course, there's no historical evidence that any of this occurred.

The Dogs-Ate-It Theory

A few modern skeptics including John Crossan, cofounder of the Jesus Seminar, have suggested that wild dogs may have eaten the body of Jesus.[16] No doubt inspired by the *my dog ate my homework* excuse frequently used in schools by noncompliant students, this theory did not surface until nearly two thousand years after the fact and has no evidence to support it.

The Body-Snatcher Theory

This theory has a number of variations depending on who the culprit is supposed to be. As we've already discussed, the suggestion that the disciples stole the body makes no sense and introduces more problems than it solves. Had the enemies of Jesus or council member Joseph of Arimathea stolen the body, you can be sure that the religious leaders would have immediately produced it in order to quell the spread of the new resurrection-based faith. And it's difficult to believe that the women could have stolen the body in light of the armed guards and four-thousand-pound rock blocking the tomb's entrance. Remember, no one fully believed the women's account of the empty tomb until they had seen the risen Christ for themselves. Once again, neither logic nor historical evidence is able to back up any of these stories.

The Hallucination Theory

It has been suggested that the disciples were so distraught over the death of their master that they all hallucinated he had come back to life. These hallucinations were apparently so real that those experiencing them believed they were actually talking, touching, and eating with the resurrected Jesus. The problem with this theory stems from the sheer number of people (over five hundred) who must share matching hallucinations. It's difficult to believe that just two people could have identical hallucinations. But in this case, not only must more than five hundred of them have the same hallucination, they must all hallucinate at the same time! And why did these mass hallucinations suddenly stop for everyone precisely forty days after they began? And to think this is the theory that has gained the most acceptance!

A Mystery Revealed

If the resurrection wasn't the springboard to get Christianity launched and sustained for all these centuries, what was? The resurrection, despite its supernatural casing, which is the primary reason for its distaste among skeptics, is simply the most plausible explanation for the origin of Christianity based on the totality of the evidence.

Simon Greenleaf, developer of the Harvard School of Law, is universally considered to be one of the most skilled legal minds this nation ever produced. After evaluating the validity of the New Testament manuscripts and its writers he concluded:

> It was therefore impossible that they could have persisted in affirming the truths they have narrated, had not Jesus actually risen from the dead, and had they not known this fact as certainly as they knew any other fact.[17]

Not only is acknowledging the resurrection as a historical fact essential in helping to understand how the Christian church began, it is crucially important for today's seekers of truth who are concerned about their eternal destiny. Those who believe in the resurrection of Jesus can face death and eternity with confidence, for we have been promised in the Scriptures that we too will receive a resurrected body just like Christ's.

> For our citizenship is in heaven, from which we also eagerly wait for the Savior, the Lord Jesus Christ, who will transform our lowly body that it may be conformed to His glorious body, according to the working by which He is able even to subdue all things to Himself. (Philippians 3:20–21)

> Behold, I tell you a mystery: We shall not all sleep, but we shall all be changed—in a moment, in the twinkling of an eye, at the last trumpet. For the trumpet will sound, and the dead will be raised incorruptible, and we shall be

changed. For this corruptible must put on incorruption, and this mortal must put on immortality. So when this corruptible has put on incorruption, and this mortal has put on immortality, then shall be brought to pass the saying that is written: "Death is swallowed up in victory." (1 Corinthians 15:51–54)

However, if the resurrection of Christ is indeed a fraud, then there is no hope for mankind. The apostle Paul explains why:

For if the dead do not rise, then Christ is not risen. And if Christ is not risen, your faith is futile; you are still in your sins! (1 Corinthians 15:16–17)

It only takes a minimum amount of faith to have eternal life. A belief in the resurrection of Christ is not all that difficult considering the amount of evidence that exists authenticating it.

If you confess with your mouth the Lord Jesus and believe in your heart that God has raised Him from the dead, you will be saved. (Romans 10:9)

Chapter Seven

LOOK HOW HE LOVES

I'm dying ... I'm dying ... I'm ...

The words were repeated again and again into the blood-spattered cell phone until there was only silence. Sarah's barely audible, frail voice trailed off before she had a chance to give the 911 operator on the other end of the line her location ...

Ringing in the New Year

For most, New Year's Day, January 1, 2008, began just as it had countless years before. Untold millions in nearly every time zone attended various festivities around the world and waited with anticipation for the clock to strike midnight. But for the family of Islamic cab driver Yaser Abdel Said of Lewisville, Texas, there were no parades or football games on this day—only horror and tragedy.

Mr. Said was an Egyptian-born Muslim who had immigrated to the

United States in 1983. At age thirty, he had married a fifteen-year-old teenager named Patricia with whom he quickly had three children—two daughters, Amina and Sarah, and a son named Islam in honor of Yaser's religion.

As his daughters grew, he became increasingly obsessed with the corrupting influence of Western culture. Using the Qur'an (Islam's holy book) as his guide, Yaser would frequently beat the girls, who would then show up at school with welts across their arms and back.[1]

To counter the abuse, both Amina and Sarah threw themselves into their schoolwork. Both were considered by their peers to be geniuses.[2] By the time Amina had reached eighteen, she had already been awarded a $20,000 scholarship for college. Meanwhile, seventeen-year-old Sarah dreamed of a job in the medical profession because she wanted to save lives.[3]

After discovering that both of his daughters had been dating non-Muslim boys from school, Yaser threatened to kill Amina and Sarah. He felt justified in making such a threat because of the Islamic teaching that Muslim women can marry only Muslim men. It would be known as an *honor killing*, which, according to the laws of Islam, allows for a Muslim man to kill any woman in the family who has *shamed* him.[4] Amina confided in a friend who later reported to police that "her dad told her he would take her back to Egypt and have her killed." Her father said, "It's OK to do that over there if you dishonor your family."[5]

On January 1, Yaser tricked his daughters into believing he was going to take them out to dinner to celebrate the New Year. He drove Sarah and Amina in his orange-colored company cab to the upscale Omni Mandalay Hotel in Irving. Before the girls could exit the car, Yaser Abdel Said turned and emptied his gun into his daughters' bodies in the name of Allah. He then left the car in the vacant taxi queue and fled the scene. The bullet-shredded bodies of Sarah and Amina were found in the cab about an hour after Sarah's desperate 911 call.[6]

Capital murder charges were immediately filed against Yaser Abdel Said and an arrest warrant issued for the fifty-year-old Muslim.[7] A few days later, Mr. Said's story appeared on the syndicated television program *America's Most Wanted*[8] and a $10,000 reward offered to anyone who could shed some light on his whereabouts.[9]

Prior to her death, Amina had posted a photo of herself on the Internet with a caption that read: "I don't want to ... become a memory." In the photo she's wearing the same tan hooded jacket that she was wearing when police discovered her lifeless body next to that of her sister's.[10]

The Law of Sharia

The United Nations estimates that there may be as many as five thousand honor killings annually around the world.[11] An actual transgression doesn't even need to be committed in order to trigger an attack; simply the *mere perception* that a woman has dishonored her family is sufficient.

Most of these killings occur in Islamic-controlled countries,[12] although immigrant communities in the United Kingdom and the United States have also shown growing signs of such occurrences.[13] Honor killing is but one form of abuse against women that stems from Sharia law. Sharia is the body of Islamic religious law that governs all practicing Muslims, regardless of the country they live in. It is based on the principles found in the Qur'an, the central religious text of Islam, and the Hadith, which is a record of the words of Muhammad, Islam's seventh-century founder.

For most of us in the West, the subjugation of women under Sharia law is difficult to comprehend. In Islam, women are thought to have brains half the size of men's.[14] In Saudi Arabia, women are not allowed to drive cars.[15] Children from divorced families are always awarded to the husband. And daughters always receive half the amount of inheritance of their brothers.[16]

Rape has become fairly commonplace in Islamic countries because proving the crime under Sharia law is for all intents and purposes impossible, since a woman's testimony is inadmissible. The actual physical act must be witnessed by four men willing to testify:

> For a woman to prove rape in Pakistan, for example, four adult males of "impeccable" character must witness the penetration, in accordance with Sharia.[17]

Another celebrated statement from the Qur'an commands husbands to literally beat their wives into submission:

> Men stand superior to women.... Those whose perverseness you fear, admonish them and remove them into bedchambers and beat them; but if they submit to you, then do not seek a way against them. (Qur'an: Surah 4:34)

Today, hundreds of millions of Muslims worldwide are demanding the formation of a one-world *Ummah* based upon Sharia law. *Ummah* is an Arabic word referring to a "collective nation of believers." The Muslim plan is to coerce all nations of the world to unite under Sharia law, which Islamic leaders perceive is the only moral solution to our present global crisis.[18] Sharia law, of course, would take precedence over any other existing laws.

As farfetched as this idea may sound, steps are already being taken in many Western nations around the world to move this "Islamic expansion" forward, under the guise of immigration and multiculturalism. In fact in July of 2008, England's most senior judge, Chief Justice Lord Phillips, ruled that Sharia law rather than English law could now be used to regulate marriage and finance within that country's Muslim communities. In an instant, the rights of women were thrust backward into the darkness of the seventh century. Muslim women living in Britain can now be legally forced into marriage, including those who are underage. They will be required to marry only Muslim men and cannot divorce their husbands, even for reasons of abuse. And if their husbands choose to divorce them, they can expect to lose custody of their children.[19]

> And so the English who gave us the Magna Carta ... and the foundation of American law are slowly succumbing to the dictates of intolerant Islam and sowing the seeds of their own destruction.... British Muslims who wish to live under Sharia Law might have stayed in the countries from which they came—or return to them. But their objective appears to be domination of England, not assimilation.... There is no due process under Sharia Law. Lord Phillips has signed the death warrant for his nation.... It's one thing to fight a war and lose it. It's quite another to willingly surrender without a struggle.[20]

Although it has become fashionable today to ignore, downplay, or criticize the role Jesus Christ has played in the formation of modern Western cultural ideals and practices, the simple fact is that our current freedoms would not exist were it not for His influence. Radical feminists who espouse vehement hatred toward Christian values would see a world today not unlike that of most Islamic countries had it not been for the teachings of Jesus. An examination of the manner in which women were treated in various ancient cultures prior to the time of Christ is needed to truly understand the impact He has had.

It's Greek to Me

Irrespective of having a reputation for philosophical superiority, the ancient Greeks nevertheless held women in extremely low regard. For example, women were not allowed to leave the house unless accompanied by a male.[21] Nor were they permitted to divorce their husbands—although men could divorce their wives at any time. And while boys were taught to read and write and were trained in the arts and in athletics, girls were deliberately kept uneducated.[22] Women were also expected never to speak in public. Famed Greek philosopher Aristotle reinforced this point when he wrote, "Silence gives grace to women."[23]

Roman women were afforded slightly more freedom than their Greek equivalents; however. they still did not share in the privileges that men enjoyed and took for granted. A low view of women was still the order of the day, and infanticide was far more common for females than males as a direct result.[24] Married women were placed under the Roman law of *manus* which gave the husband complete control and ownership of her and her possessions.[25] Under *manus*, a woman could not legally inherit property. Nor could she divorce her husband, although again, he could divorce her. And as with the Greeks, Roman women were not allowed to speak in public settings or testify in court.

Perhaps the most harrowing limitation of a woman's freedom stemmed from the Fourth Table of the Twelve Tables of Roman Law. This set of rules known as *patria potestas* gave the man absolute power over his wife and children and even extended into the area of life and death, which meant a husband could have his wife or child executed if he so desired. Historian Rudolph Sohm, writing in *The Institutes of Roman Law* in 1892, explains:

> [The husband had] full authority to chastise [physically beat] his wife, and, in some cases, even to kill her, in the same way as he might chastise or kill his child.[26]

These laws, which had their beginnings in the fifth century BC, were still in vogue by the year 18 BC when Caesar Augustus reinforced them by issuing *lex Julia de adulteriis*—a law that encouraged husbands to have their wives or daughters executed if they were found to have engaged in the act of adultery.[27] Of course, husbands were not subject to the same standard. Men could take their mistresses out in public without having to worry about the threat of death or even raising an eyebrow, for that matter.

But all that soon changed …

All Things Made New

The concept that women were intellectually and socially inferior to men—an idea that had been passed down from generation to generation for hundreds, if not thousands, of years—was suddenly turned upside down by the arrival of Jesus Christ.

> There is neither Jew nor Greek, there is neither slave nor free, there is neither male nor female; for you are all one in Christ Jesus. (Galatians 3:28)

gation

The above biblical passage makes it clear that all people regardless of their race, class, or sex were considered equal in the eyes of Christ. No one before Jesus had ever attempted to present such a concept. Scholar L. F. Cervantes wrote in the late 1960s, a time when the feminist movement in America was beginning to heat up, that, "The birth of Jesus was the turning point in the history of women."[28]

Take for example the respect Jesus showed the Samaritan woman He met at the well:

> A woman of Samaria came to draw water. Jesus said to her, "Give Me a drink." For His disciples had gone away into the city to buy food. Then the woman of Samaria said to Him, "How is it that You, being a Jew, ask a drink from me, a Samaritan woman?" For Jews have no dealings with Samaritans. Jesus answered and said to her, "If you knew the gift of God, and who it is who says to you, 'Give Me a drink,' you would have asked Him, and He would have given you living water." (John 4:7–10)

While this encounter may not seem terribly unusual to us today in our modern Western culture, you must understand that at *that* particular time in history, such an exchange would have been unthinkable. Not only was Jesus speaking to a dreaded Samaritan, He was speaking to an actual woman in public! After returning from town, Jesus' disciples were shocked by what they saw:

> And at this point His disciples came, and they marveled that He talked with a woman. (John 4:27)

Not only was Jesus going against the cultural grain by speaking to women in public, He had the audacity to teach them about spiritual matters as well. The rabbinical tradition from three hundred years earlier recorded in the Talmud stated: *Let the words of the Law be burned rather than committed to a woman.*[29] Women were not to be trusted with the knowledge of spiritual concepts. Yet Jesus had no qualms about violating such customs.

The apostle John records an encounter between Jesus and Martha in which He presents the crux of the gospel to her. It is the only time this important dialogue appears anywhere in the Bible. By reserving one of His most important speeches for her, Jesus erased centuries of bias against women by showing just how much He valued her soul …

> Jesus said to her, "I am the resurrection and the life. He who believes in Me, though he may die, he shall live. And whoever lives and believes in Me shall never die. Do you believe this?" She said to Him, "Yes, Lord, I believe that You are the Christ, the Son of God, who is to come into the world." (John 11:25–27)

An Important Role

As previously mentioned, the resurrection of Christ is the cornerstone of the Christian faith. And yet, it was *a group of women* who discovered and announced to the world what is arguably one of the most crucial events in all of history. Although He could have just as easily appeared to John or Peter, who also visited His tomb that Sunday morning, Jesus instead chose to make Himself known to Mary Magdalene along with a group of women that included Mary, Joanna, Salome, and others.

Remember, the culture of the time dictated that a woman could not speak publicly. Nor could a woman be used as an eyewitness. Yet

here, Jesus was counting on these women to fulfill both tasks. Jesus'
high regard for the dignity of women would soon begin to infiltrate
the surrounding culture and would eventually spread throughout the
Western world.

Following the resurrection of Christ, the church began to grow at a
phenomenal pace. Women who had previously been barred from attending
spiritual services quickly began to freely participate. In fact, women actually outnumbered men in the early church.[30] The New Testament records
the names of a number of women including Lydia, Apphia, Priscilla, and
Phoebe, who became key leaders within the church.

Church historians recognize that women were highly active in the
early church—often more so than men—and were very much responsible
for helping it to grow at the pace that it did.[31] Jesus had broken the bonds
that for centuries had defined women as second-class citizens.

Marital Freedom

Jesus treated the women He encountered with respect, dignity, esteem,
and care; and most importantly, as men's equal. Based on this precept,
the apostle Paul wrote something in his letter to the Ephesian church that
forever changed the relationship between husbands and wives and elevated
the status of women to a level previously unknown in history.

> Husbands, love your wives, just as Christ also loved the
> church and gave Himself for her. (Ephesians 5:25)

For the first time, men were told that their wives were worth
dying for. This was positively unheard of. Women were used to being

threatened, beaten, secluded, and controlled. Now their husbands were being asked, through the teachings of Christ, to treat their wives as equals.

The words and deeds of Jesus regarding the manner in which husbands and wives should relate to each other were, of course, perfectly in sync with God's original design. In the book of Genesis, it is recorded that man and woman were *both* created in the image of God as male and female.[32] Therefore, both are equally deserving of the same dignity and respect. Although they may have vastly different roles and responsibilities, neither is superior to the other.

Men who were followers of Christ could no longer, in good conscience, keep their wives secluded or threaten to have them beaten. The teachings and examples of Jesus had proven to be so successful that by the year 374 AD, Emperor Valentinian had the law of *patria potestas* repealed, which effectively ended more than a thousand years of legal female suppression.[33]

Two Many Wives

The laws and culture of the ancient Greeks and Romans did not allow men to have more than one wife. However, this was merely a technicality since most of them had, or at least were encouraged to have, mistresses on the side. Other societies at that time, most notably those in the Middle East, did allow for multiple marriages. Polygamy even found its way into the Hebrew culture as illustrated by a number of Old Testament patriarchs including Abraham, David, and Solomon, all of whom had a multiplicity of wives. Usually this was done for the purpose of moving the childbearing process forward more quickly.

Polygamy was still acceptable by the time Jesus arrived in the Middle East. However, He always spoke of marriage in the context of one man and one woman. According to Christ, marriage was for two—not more than two:

> For this reason a man shall leave his father and mother and be joined to his wife, and the *two* shall become one flesh. So then, they are no longer *two* but one flesh. (Matthew 19:5–6)

Jesus' defense of monogamy was not only in keeping with His high view of women (who ultimately found the practice of polygamy humiliating), but also God's original design for man and woman as depicted in the garden of Eden.[34] As Christianity began to spread across the globe, the practice of polygamy began to fade—except of course in those areas of the world where Christianity was not readily accepted. There was, however, one peculiar exception.

Polygamy played a major role during the formation of the Mormon church in the United States in the mid-1800s. Early on, founder Joseph Smith had received a "divine revelation" from an "angelic being" commanding him to take additional wives, or so he claimed ... which no doubt came as a shock to his then wife, Emma. Subsequent Mormon leaders, including Brigham Young and others, would enthusiastically follow suit in the ensuing days.[35] Although claiming to be a Christian denomination of sorts, Mormonism actually parallels the Muslim religion far more closely—especially in terms of their view of males having sex with multiple female partners in the hereafter.

In 1896, the Mormon-controlled state of Utah was finally granted entrance into the Union, but only after agreeing to outlaw polygamous marriages. This incident provided another example of how Christ's teachings (pertaining to the definition of marriage) had permeated the foundation of U.S. law just as it had in other Western cultures. Today, with the so-called divine directive to practice polygamy rescinded, the Mormon church no longer officially advocates such behavior. However, there are reports of tens of thousands of Mormon fundamentalists in Utah (those who adhere to the strict teachings of the religion's founders) who continue to take multiple wives in secret—believing that it is a necessary requirement for entrance into the celestial kingdom.[36]

A Muslim Encounter

Recently, I spoke at a large church in one of the western states in the U.S. The topic that morning was similar to some of the concepts that are being presented in this book. While listing a few of the many unique virtues of Jesus, I mentioned that He had done more than any other person to lift the status of women. I then gave some examples. At the conclusion of the service I asked if there were any in the audience who wanted to ask Jesus into their lives. A very confident and beautiful Middle Eastern–looking woman was one of the first to come forward. I immediately discovered that she had been a Muslim all of her life. She wore the typical Islamic attire, but it was much more fashionable and colorful than I was used to seeing. She said assuredly, "Dr. LaHaye, I want to receive your God. I want to be free from the repression of Islam." Prior to this Sunday morning service, her neighbors had been telling her about Jesus and had encouraged her to come to church with them. By the end of the service, her heart was ready to accept the Lord.

This incident reminded me of one of the essential concepts of Islam that relates to women. I had been wondering for years why any woman would actually want to be a Muslim. For in addition to the repression they suffer in this life, they have an afterlife to look forward to consisting of nothing more than being one of a group of women who are required to satisfy the sexual whims of their assigned Muslim male ... for all eternity! It's no wonder this woman was anxious to get to know the God of the Bible and the freedom only He can bring.

Hard as it might be for some to believe, it is the Muslim teaching regarding sex in the afterlife that was primarily responsible for the deaths of three thousand innocent people in New York, Washington DC, and Pennsylvania on September 11, 2001. Clearly, the nineteen male Islamic terrorists that day expected to wake up from their fiery deaths in the next life surrounded by countless virgins waiting to satisfy their every sexual desire. This is what they had been taught since childhood would be their reward for killing Christians, Jews, and Americans in the name of Allah. Men who continue to blow themselves up in various cities in the Middle East on an almost daily basis are similarly motivated.[37]

I have stayed in touch with the pastor of this church and have continued to receive updates regarding this woman's progress in her new life. According to the pastor, she is doing quite well—attending Bible study on a regular basis and growing steadily in her relationship with the Lord. She is also filled with an obvious new sense of joy. But hers will not be an easy road. Depending on the level of outward expression of her new faith, she can expect at the very least to be ostracized from certain members of her family, and at the most, may even find her life in danger. This is, in fact, a very real possibility since her "crime" against Allah—professing Jesus as her personal Savior—is considered to be far more serious than the "crime" that was committed by Sarah and Amina Said.

Advocate of the Oppressed

The love that Jesus demonstrated to those around Him did not stop with His elevation and honoring of women. From the beginning, Jesus was an advocate of the less fortunate. The prophet Isaiah had forecast the ministry of the Messiah seven hundred years before His appearance with the following words:

> "The Spirit of the LORD God is upon Me, because the Lord has anointed Me to preach good tidings to the poor; He has sent Me to heal the brokenhearted, to proclaim liberty to the captives, and the opening of the prison to those who are bound; to proclaim the acceptable year of the Lord." (Isaiah 61:1–2)

Jesus claimed for Himself the role of Messiah after publicly reading this passage of Scripture aloud and then stating, "Today, this Scripture is fulfilled in your hearing" (Luke 4:21). It is significant that He stopped this prophetic mission statement with the words "to proclaim the acceptable year of the Lord" (Luke 4:19), which meant that His ministry during the current church age would focus on acts of mercy and love.

At one point, Jesus boiled down the entire list of God's commandments to just two—loving God with all your heart and loving your neighbor (see Luke 10:27). The commandment to love your neighbor incorporated His redefinition of what constituted a neighbor—which included anyone who was in need, especially those considered to be social outcasts:

> But when you give a feast, invite the poor, the maimed, the lame, the blind. And you will be blessed, because they

cannot repay you; for you shall be repaid at the resurrection of the just. (Luke 14:13–14)

Jesus continually discussed the necessity to help those less fortunate by
emphasizing the point that eternal rewards awaited those who wisely chose
to act upon His words:

> "I was hungry and you gave Me food; I was thirsty and
> you gave Me drink; I was a stranger and you took Me
> in; I was naked and you clothed Me; I was sick and you
> visited Me; I was in prison and you came to Me." Then
> the righteous will answer Him, saying, "Lord, when did
> we see You hungry and feed You, or thirsty and give You
> drink? When did we see You a stranger and take You in,
> or naked and clothe You? Or when did we see You sick, or
> in prison, and come to You?" And the King will answer
> and say to them, "Assuredly, I say to you, inasmuch as
> you did it to one of the least of these My brethren, you
> did it to Me." (Matthew 25:35–40)

For the Bible Tells Me So

Recently I encountered a country-western guitarist named Kenny, a giant
of a man who stood six foot five without his cowboy boots. As a volunteer
for various prison ministries, Kenny had played in some of the toughest
prisons in the nation.

One evening, he recounted how he had once been assigned to perform in the "lockdown" section of a particularly tough prison. Upon

his arrival, the prisoners began loudly chanting "Music! Music! Music!" while pounding their fists on anything that would make noise. The escorting guards unlocked the entrance just far enough for the singer and his guitar to squeeze through, and then slammed the door shut and locked it behind him. Kenny suddenly found himself in the most frightening and hostile environment he'd ever been in.

An atmosphere of hatred permeated the room. This interracial group of inmates looked as if they were ready to take their anger and frustration out on anyone they could find, and Kenny was their closest target. One prisoner stared at Kenny with piercing eyes that seemed to say, "If I get my hands on you, it's all over!"

While strumming a few basic chords on his guitar, Kenny sent up a silent prayer to his heavenly Father, *"Lord, what do You want me to say to these men?"* Before he knew it, he was singing the words to a simple children's song:

Jesus loves me! This I know,
For the Bible tells me so.
Little ones to Him belong.
They are weak but He is strong.
Yes, Jesus loves me!
Yes, Jesus loves me!
Yes, Jesus loves me!
The Bible tells me so.

The moment he finished, the chanting and pounding immediately resumed; only this time they were calling for Kenny to sing it again! During the second run-through, a number of men began to quietly sing along. To Kenny's utter amazement, even the hate-filled man who had stared at him earlier was mouthing the words, "Yes, Jesus loves me." And when it was all over, many of the inmates had tears glistening on their cheeks.

Realizing that God was breaking through these hardened hearts, Kenny began to tell his own story—how he had accepted Jesus into his life at his mother's knee when he was seven; how he had made a lot of bad choices while traveling the entertainment circuit; how he had practiced every sin represented by the men in this prison; and how after ruining his life he had called out to God asking for forgiveness, and discovering that his Creator still loved him.

A number of men that afternoon humbled themselves before God and received Christ into their lives—to the absolute astonishment of the prison guards. Many of these men were confronted for the first time that there was indeed a God in heaven who loved them and who had a plan for their lives. Others, like Kenny, had been Christians early on who had turned their backs on God so they could indulge in a self-dominated life that included drugs, crime, and unspeakable deeds.

> If we say that we have no sin, we deceive ourselves, and the truth is not in us. If we confess our sins, He is faithful and just to forgive us our sins and to cleanse us from all unrighteousness. (1 John 1:8–9)

It is my belief that many of those who live a rebellious life of sin do so because they have never been told about or truly experienced the incredible love God has for all mankind and for them as individuals. Rare is it indeed that a gross sinner has been aware of or understood God's love. This is what makes Christianity unique over the man-made religions of the world; for it is based upon the greatest demonstration of love ever made.

Loving Your Enemies

Jesus, of course, knew that the greatest force in the universe was love, and He continually demonstrated that concept while He was on the earth. God's love and the love of His Son are exclusive to Christianity. Most other religions of the world are based on fear. Islam, for example, the second-largest religion in the world next to Christianity, is one such religion. As we've seen, its scriptures encourage hatred and violence by commanding its followers to "kill all infidels"—those who refuse to bow down to Allah or his prophet Muhammad. An unbiased examination of the historic life of the seventh-century Muhammad is a study in murder, mayhem, and slaughter. By contrast, Jesus Christ taught His disciples to love, even going so far as to recommend they "love their enemies"!

> You have heard that it was said, "You shall love your neighbor and hate your enemy." But I say to you, love your enemies, bless those who curse you, do good to those who hate you, and pray for those who spitefully use you and persecute you. (Matthew 5:43–44)

If the world had followed just that one teaching of Jesus, think of the billions of innocent lives that could have been spared throughout the ages in all of our wars. Yet despite the logic and brilliance of such a commandment, man continues to kill, torture, persecute, and enslave his fellow man.

Incomprehensible Love

> For God so loved the world that He gave His only
> begotten Son, that whoever believes in Him should not
> perish but have everlasting life. (John 3:16)

It has been said that this is the most famous (and most beloved) verse in the entire Bible. I have been at their bedside and watched as several people have slipped through the doorway of eternity into God's wonderful future with those blessed words on their lips. Sometimes they were so weak they could only silently mouth those words of promise as they "escaped the bonds of this earth." Many nonbelievers have turned to Christ once they have been confronted with the incredible truth that God loves them and has from the time of their creation. The proof of that love lies in the fact that He gave His Son as a sacrifice for our sins so that we could be reconciled to Him and have eternal life:

> In this the love of God was manifested toward us, that
> God has sent His only begotten Son into the world,
> that we might live through Him. In this is love, not
> that we loved God, but that He loved us and sent His
> Son to be the propitiation for our sins. Beloved, if God
> so loved us, we also ought to love one another. (1 John
> 4:9–11)

I once explained the gospel to a talkative atheist as we sat next to each other on an airplane. Afterward, he said, "I don't see how one man's blood could wash away the sins of all the people who have ever lived." To his amazement, I agreed with him saying, "You're right, one man's blood couldn't even cleanse his own sin, let alone thirteen billion others." But this is why the identity of Jesus Christ is so important. You see, if Jesus was just the biological product of Joseph and Mary, he wouldn't qualify as an adequate covering for sin. However, if He is the virgin-born Son of God who was able to avoid the sin curse of Adam by not having a biological father, He would indeed be God in human form, which is exactly how the Bible describes Him. His suffering and death on the cross would most certainly be able to permanently cleanse all who have ever lived from their sins. This is by far the greatest expression of love ever demonstrated.

> Christ Jesus, who, being in the form of God, did not consider it robbery to be equal with God, but made Himself of no reputation, taking the form of a bond-servant, and coming in the likeness of men. And being found in appearance as a man, He humbled Himself and became obedient to the point of death, even the death of the cross. (Philippians 2:5–8)

If Jesus had even one speck of sin within Him, He never would have qualified as a universal sacrifice. But the fact that He was raised from the dead on the third day demonstrates that God approved of His sacrifice. The entire message of Christianity rests on the sinlessness of Jesus Christ.

> For He made Him who knew no sin to be sin for us,
> that we might become the righteousness of God in Him.
> (2 Corinthians 5:21)

It has been my privilege to visit Israel thirteen times during my lifetime. A number of places in and around Jerusalem are truly inspirational—such as the Garden Tomb where Jesus rose from the dead, or the Mount of Olives where Jesus gave His tremendous prophetic discourse about the *end times*. It was here that He also issued His Great Commission, which encouraged His church to go into all the world and preach the gospel. However, the place that actually brought me to tears and resulted in the rededication of my life to Christ was the garden of Gethsemane. Our guide explained that some of the surrounding olive trees were twenty-five hundred years old, which means that they could have been silent witnesses to the actions of Jesus as He entered into an agony of prayer:

> He knelt down and prayed, saying, "Father, if it is Your will, take this cup away from Me; nevertheless not My will, but Yours, be done." Then an angel appeared to Him from heaven, strengthening Him. And being in agony, He prayed more earnestly. Then His sweat became like great drops of blood falling down to the ground. (Luke 22:41–44)

Jesus was not trying to dodge the crucifixion, which He knew was right around the corner. But He knew He would have to take upon Himself every sin ever committed by anyone—past, present, and future—every rape, murder, lie, robbery, and child molestation. He also knew that this would separate Him from His Father for the first and only time. Not only that, His Father in heaven would have to stand by and allow His Son to die an excruciating death. This was our Lord's darkest hour. But He went through with it because of His boundless love for us, in spite of our sin and rebellion against Him. No wonder hymn writer Frederick Lehman was moved to pen the following:

The love of God is greater far
Than tongue or pen can ever tell;
It goes beyond the highest star,
And reaches to the lowest hell;
The guilty pair, bowed down with care,
God gave His Son to win;
His erring child He reconciled,
And pardoned from his sin.

O love of God, how rich and pure!
How measureless and strong!
It shall forevermore endure
The saints' and angels' song.

God the Father and His only begotten Son love you and want you to enjoy being in the family of God. Some will say, "But I don't deserve to be in God's family." Well, neither do I! But Jesus Christ loved us so much that He died and rose again to save us. I cannot improve on the immortal words of the apostle Paul, who stated:

> Who shall separate us from the love of Christ? Shall tribu-
> lation, or distress, or persecution, or famine, or nakedness,
> or peril, or sword?… Yet in all these things we are more
> than conquerors through Him who loved us. For I am
> persuaded that neither death nor life, nor angels nor
> principalities nor powers, nor things present nor things to
> come, nor height nor depth, nor any other created thing,
> shall be able to separate us from the love of God which is
> in Christ Jesus our Lord. (Romans 8:35, 37–39)

Chapter Eight

THEY STILL DON'T KNOW
WHAT THEY ARE DOING

In 1945, while digging around some caves near the town of Nag
Hammadi in Egypt, an Egyptian peasant is said to have discovered a large
earthenware vessel buried in the sand. Inside were twelve leather-bound
papyrus codices (books) dating back to the third and fourth centuries.
Written in the Coptic language, the manuscripts were comprised of fifty-
two primarily Gnostic-themed treatises—the most notable one being a
nearly complete text of what has become known as the "lost" Gospel of
Thomas.[1]

Over the next few decades, the contents of these texts, dubbed the
Nag Hammadi library, would be translated into numerous languages and
gradually released to the public. Little did anyone know that a major
revival of sorts was about to take place.

Laying the Groundwork

Elaine Pagels, professor of religion at Princeton University in New Jersey, was studying for her PhD at Harvard in 1969 when she suddenly found herself on the team analyzing the Nag Hammadi manuscripts. This experience eventually led her to write the best seller *The Gnostic Gospels* a decade later. The book went on to win both the National Book Award and National Book Critics Circle Award and was chosen by the Modern Library as one of the 100 best nonfiction books of the twentieth century.[2] Notwithstanding, the Intercollegiate Studies Institute also listed it as one of the fifty worst books of the twentieth century.[3]

In 1982, mystic Michael Baigent, along with coauthors Richard Leigh and Henry Lincoln, released the book *Holy Blood, Holy Grail*. The controversial international best seller put forth the Gnostic hypothesis that Jesus and Mary Magdalene had been married and had spawned one or more children whose descendants eventually immigrated to France. Although Baigent and company presented their conspiracy theories and ancient mysteries as fact, academic historians felt the book should have been classified as *pseudohistorical* due to its speculative and inadequately sourced nature.[4] Nevertheless, these same concepts would be successfully borrowed and fictionalized twenty years later by author Dan Brown in his infamous thriller, *The Da Vinci Code*, in which he even references Baigent's work by name.[5]

On June 26, 2000, ABC News aired a two-hour prime-time special titled *The Search for Jesus* hosted by the late Peter Jennings. The controversial program was greeted with high ratings and complimentary reviews from critics. However, viewers tuning into the program looking for an unbiased, newsworthy presentation of historic truths pertaining to Jesus had their hopes dashed within the first few minutes.

More than half of the "experts" interviewed by Jennings were members of Funk and Crossan's antibiblical Jesus Seminar organization. The rest were likewise liberal and weak in their presentation of Bible-related information, with one token biblical scholar edited out of context in order to support ABC's predetermined plan to undermine historical Christianity in front of their tens of millions of viewers. Jennings's narration, not surprisingly, sympathized with those from the Jesus Seminar.[6]

During the course of the program, the following major Gnostic themes were presented as fact:

1. Traditional Christian beliefs are not based on evidence.
2. The four gospels contradict each other and it is unclear who actually wrote them.
3. Jesus was an illegitimate child. He was not born in Bethlehem nor was His mother, Mary, a virgin.
4. Jesus did not perform miracles. His acts of healing were psychosomatic in nature.
5. The betrayal of Jesus by Judas (whose name means "Jew") should be classified as anti-Semitic fiction.
6. Jesus did not die for the world's sins.
7. Jesus was buried in a shallow grave, not in a tomb. His unresurrected body was most likely eaten by wild dogs.

The obvious intention of the program was to undermine historic Christianity at every level, including the all-important resurrection of Christ. Peter Jennings, however, was smart enough to know that Christianity would not have survived this long were it not for the resurrection, and even stated something to that effect on the program:

> The mystery religions and their gods lost all credibility centuries ago. Not so with the resurrection of Jesus. His

followers stuck to their story even though they were per-
secuted, and as we know, the Jesus movement grew and
flourished, which is why some eminent scholars believe
there was indeed a resurrection.[7]

Notice that Jennings never admits the resurrection actually took
place—only that some scholars *believe* it did because the disciples stub-
bornly "stuck to their story."

The groundwork was laid. Numerous other Gnostic-oriented books
and television specials were in the pipeline, ready to be unleashed on
an unsuspecting public. The stage was now set to carry the snowballing
Gnostic revival into the twenty-first century.

A Banner Year

As it turns out, 2003 proved to be a banner year for the mainstreaming
of ancient Gnosticism. On March 18 of that year, *The Da Vinci Code* by
Dan Brown was released and immediately shot to the top of the *New
York Times* fiction best-seller list during its first week before the public—a
truly amazing feat for an obscure author. A year later, the book was still
selling between 80,000 and 90,000 copies per week and was already in its
fifty-sixth printing![8]

Also in 2003, Elaine Pagels released her follow-up to *The Gnostic
Gospels* titled *Beyond Belief: The Secret Gospel of Thomas*. In this *New York
Times* nonfiction best seller, Pagels attempted to thoroughly discredit
John's gospel while simultaneously elevating the Gnostic Gospel of
Thomas above that of the Bible.[9]

Eight months after the release of *The Da Vinci Code*, ABC News aired a prime-time television special titled *Jesus, Mary, and Da Vinci* which suggested that some of the themes in the book may not have been so fictional after all. Emphasizing the point, Dan Brown appeared on ABC's *Good Morning America* program earlier that same day stating that he might not have changed any of the historical material had the book been nonfiction.[10] Sales of *The Da Vinci Code* soared following ABC's remarkable one-two promotional punch.

Not to be outdone, NBC's *Dateline* aired *The Mystery of the Jesus Papers* in April of 2006. The program began with the question, "What if everything you know about Jesus is wrong?" As previously noted, guest Michael Baigent boldly asserted during his interview that what the general populace thinks it knows about Jesus is "an obvious lie."[11]

In May of 2006, the film version of *The Da Vinci Code* starring Tom Hanks opened worldwide and became the week's top-grossing film, taking in more than $77 million in the U.S. alone.[12] Sony's ad campaign promised viewers that if they came to the movie, they would "uncover the greatest mystery of all time."[13] And just what was the mystery? That Jesus and Mary Magdalene were married and had conceived a child.

During the first seven years of the new millennium, Jesus Christ appeared on the covers of *Time, Newsweek,* and *U.S. News & World Report* magazines a combined total of nearly twenty times. As previously noted, almost all of the accompanying articles reflected the same Gnostic themes shared by the above-mentioned books, movies, and television specials.

While the specifics of this ongoing Gnostic media blitz differ from article to article, book to book, or program to program, the conclusions are always the same ... the Bible is wrong, Jesus is not deity, and much of Christianity is a lie. What's more, these carefully crafted, one-sided presentations are not intended for the scholars or theologians of the world, where the merits of such theories can be intellectually debated, scrutinized, and held up to the light of manuscript or archeological evidence. No, their intention is simply to influence the general populace. Bypassing the normal route of historical investigation, these ancient Gnostic concepts repackaged for a twenty-first-century culture are marketed directly to the masses. Their goal is to discourage, create doubt, and ultimately foster confusion and hopelessness not only in believers, but in those sincerely seeking after the truth.

Extreme Makeover: Gnostic Edition

Gnostics believe their texts represent the real core of Christian truth as originally conceived, but due to the "sinister institution of the organized church" this truth has been concealed from the public. Therefore, what most Christians hold today as biblical truth, they say, is a flawed invention that has managed to suppress the "real truth" of Gnosticism for twenty centuries. If the contents of these Gnostic documents are indeed true, then a thorough makeover of Christianity is surely needed. But are they true?

Gnostic proponents claim that all historians, theologians, and believers down through the centuries have been duped, and that the millions of lives around the world that have been dramatically changed for the better as a result of a faith in Christ have been a mistake. The inspiration behind the world's greatest works of art; the motivation to build hospitals; the humanitarian assistance provided by Christian groups; the elevation of women resulting from Christ's teachings; the archeological evidence for the Bible on display in the museums of the world; the reverence for Jesus—could all this be the result of one big, deceptive conspiracy?

Since the primary claims of Gnosticism today are diametrically opposed to everything Christians hold dear, it is imperative to know which viewpoint holds the keys to the truth. The critical question is … did Gnosticism precede Christianity as the Gnostics claim, or is it the other way around? Did the followers of traditional Christianity succeed in suppressing the "alternative Christianity" of Gnosticism?

It is generally accepted that Jesus' ministry took place in the early AD 30s. Those who were closest to Him, the apostles, documented their experiences and eyewitness accounts in writing. All of the manuscripts that make up the New Testament were written during the first century beginning in the 50s or possibly earlier, with the final text, the prophetic book of Revelation, penned during the early to mid 90s by the apostle John in his old age while imprisoned on the Isle of Patmos.

Gnostic texts, on the other hand, would not come into being until the second century, although those who promote them today have tried their best to argue for earlier dates for these manuscripts.[14] The reason is because the closer the creation of a manuscript is to the event it discusses, the more weight it carries.

Dr. Craig Evans, professor of New Testament at Arcadia Divinity College in Nova Scotia, was appalled to find pro-Gnostic scholars trying to fudge the dates of various Gnostic manuscripts while working on a documentary for National Geographic:

> There is a stealth scholarship at work. What I've noticed is this tendency to take what clearly are second-century if not later sources and sneak them into an earlier period— to try to get the Gospel of Thomas and the Gospel of Mary or maybe even the Gospel of Judas and smuggle those later documents as close to the end of the first century as possible. And then you will hear them in reference to the New Testament gospels and other New Testament

writings doing just the opposite—pushing them further away as close to the end of the first century, maybe even in some cases into the beginning of the second century, so that they can then begin to speak very loosely of early "Christian" writings. And that's the part about it that I find frustrating.[15]

The texts that ultimately formed the foundation of traditional Christianity were all written soon after the occurrence of the events they describe. Not only that, they were recorded by those who were best qualified to write them—the eyewitnesses. In addition, the manuscripts were quickly circulated and discussed in the surrounding regions while other witnesses were still alive who could object to any inaccurate content. The same cannot be said for the Gnostic manuscripts, which wouldn't be written until the second, third, and fourth centuries—plenty of time to develop an alternate take on the life of Christ, especially with all the eyewitnesses now long gone.[16]

During the second century, those who were in rebellion against the Christian faith, which included writers such as Basilides, Carpocrates, Saturninus, and Valentinus, penned their own versions of the story of Christ. The Gospel of Peter, the Gospel of the Ebionites, the Gospel of the Egyptians, and of course, the Gospel of Thomas are examples of such manuscripts. Other works with titles such as the Gospel of Philip, the Gospel of Mary Magdalene, the Gospel of the Savior, the Apocryphon of John, the Apocalypse of Peter, and the Hypostasis of the Archons followed in succeeding centuries.

Justin Martyr was the first early writer to devote himself almost exclusively to defending the Christian faith against the swelling tide of such heresies. His first work, *Apology Volume 1*, appeared in AD 155 (*apology* is a Greek word meaning *in defense of* and should not be confused with the English definition of *being sorry for*). The Gnostic desire to change and alter the events involving the life of Christ and the content of His teachings was one of the motivating factors behind Martyr's aspiration to compose detailed evaluations of this alternative movement.

Other apologists soon followed in the footsteps of Justin Martyr, including Irenaeus, Tertullian, Clement of Alexandria, and Origen. By the third century, a massive amount of data from these sources had been compiled that validated the accuracy of the New Testament Scriptures while simultaneously showing the historical and factual inaccuracies of the Gnostic writings.

Included within this time period is the infamous meeting that took place in Nicaea in AD 325, under the direction of the Roman emperor Constantine. Gnostic adherents usually cry foul over Nicaea since they claim this is where it was determined which books would ultimately be included in the Bible.[17] They question, for example, why the gospel of John was included and not the Gospel of Thomas; or why the book of Revelation was chosen and not the Hypostasis of the Archons. Modern Gnostic promoters have since adopted the belief that an ancient conspiracy to suppress their views was already under way—a conspiracy that has somehow succeeded in keeping the truths of Gnosticism from the world.

It's All John's Fault

In her book *Beyond Belief: The Secret Gospel of Thomas*, author Elaine Pagels squarely puts the blame for the suppression of Gnosticism on the apostle John:

> Many Christians today who read the Gospel of Thomas assume at first that it is simply wrong, and deservedly called

heretical. Yet what Christians have disparagingly called
Gnostic and heretical sometimes turn out to be forms
of Christian teaching that are merely unfamiliar to us—
unfamiliar precisely because of the active and successful
opposition of Christians such as John.[18]

According to Pagels, the grand conspiracy against Gnosticism began
with the apostle John, whom the New Testament Scriptures identify as *the
disciple whom Jesus loved*. John obviously held a special place in Jesus' heart
and was included in Christ's most unique events such as the transfiguration. It was John who sat next to and rested against Jesus during the Last
Supper. And it was John who was the first disciple to believe Jesus had
been resurrected after running to the tomb on the morning of the resurrection and finding it empty, save for the grave clothes.[19]

For Pagels to target John of all people as the one most responsible for
distorting the truth about Jesus (which ultimately led to the so-called greatest
cover-up in the history of the world) is truly misguided at best. John was
clearly in one of the best positions possible to accurately document what he
had seen. To understand why she would single out John, we must realize that
all of his New Testament writings demonstrate a concern for the nature of
Christ—confirming that He was indeed unique among men, the Messiah,
the Son of God, deity in human flesh. And it is this emphasis that renders
John's writings totally incompatible with today's Gnostic perspective.

A Defining Moment

What makes defining Gnosticism difficult is the presence of conflicting
views within the category itself. For example, some believe that Jesus did

not die on the cross but simply passed out and was later resuscitated. Others believe that Jesus did die on the cross and His body was subsequently stolen. Although both theories are in conflict with one another and cannot both be true, they nevertheless are both classified as Gnostic since they deny the reality of the resurrection.

Some historians have attempted to sift through the contradictory ideas that make up Gnosticism to try to solidify some sort of foundational theology for it, and have come up with three basic points—all of which are in direct opposition to accepted Judeo-Christian theology.

1. Gnosticism encompasses the idea that god has two distinct personas—the good, unknowable, transcendent god; and the evil, knowable, creator god.
2. Creation contains both good and evil within Gnosticism. The creator caused certain aspects of the creation to be evil from the beginning. Light, spirit, and knowledge represent what is good, while darkness, matter, flesh, and ignorance represent all that is evil.
3. Salvation comes about through secret knowledge. And while the spirit is redeemable, the flesh is not. Therefore, within Gnosticism, there is no such thing as the resurrection of the body.[20]

Based on the above definition, it's clear that Gnosticism not only clashes with traditional Christianity on its most important aspect, the resurrection, it also rejects the entire basis of the Old Testament because of its peculiar view of the nature of the creator god as being evil. With its basic "theology" in opposition to Judeo-Christian tradition, and with Gnosticism's desire to simultaneously be syncretistic (that is, merge its beliefs with those of other religions), one can see the dangers facing Christian believers of the second and third centuries. It's no wonder that the apologists were so keen to clarify the Christian position and keep it from becoming diluted or corrupted by Gnosticism's philosophical worldview.

Doubts about Thomas

A nearly intact Gospel of Thomas was one of the manuscripts found at Nag Hammadi. For those who may not be familiar with this document, it is not really a gospel at all, despite its title, but a collection of 114 unrelated sayings that have been randomly strung together and attributed to Jesus.[21] There is no narrative story about any events involving Jesus or His disciples. The figure that emerges from this manuscript is an alternate Jesus, whose character is not clearly defined. Is he human, is he divine, or both?

The Gospel of Thomas is usually given special attention by the Gnostic community for two reasons: They claim it can be dated earlier than other Gnostic texts (but still not as early as the original New Testament manuscripts), and it portrays Jesus as a wise, sagelike guru. In recent times, however, even the early dating of Thomas has been called into question. Many scholars now believe that the manuscript originated in Syria sometime after the end of the second century.[22]

A number of its statements appear to have been pulled from the New Testament texts that were originally written by the apostles and changed slightly in order to give them a Gnostic flair. Consider the following:

> The disciples said to Jesus: "Tell us whom the kingdom
> of heaven is like!" He said to them: "It is like a mustard
> seed. It is the smallest of all seeds. But when it falls on

cultivated soil, it produces a large branch (and) becomes shelter for birds of the sky." (The Gnostic Gospel of Thomas, Saying #20)[23]

Jesus says: "If two make peace with one another in one and the same house, (then) they will say to the mountain: 'Move away,' and it will move away." (The Gnostic Gospel of Thomas, Saying #48)[24]

The two sayings above both use well-known imagery (the mustard seed and the moving mountain) taken from the words of Jesus as they appear in the New Testament. However, notice how the original subject of *faith* has been removed from the passages (see Matthew 17:20; Mark 11:23; Luke 17:6) so as to completely alter the meaning of the texts.

Jesus said to his disciples: "Compare me and tell me whom I am like." Simon Peter said to him: "You are like a just messenger." Matthew said to him: "You are like an (especially) wise philosopher." Thomas said to him: "Teacher, my mouth cannot bear at all to say whom you are like." Jesus said: "I am not your teacher. For you have drunk, you have become intoxicated at the bubbling spring that I have measured out." And he took him, (and) withdrew, (and) he said three words to him. But when Thomas came back to his companions, they asked him: "What did Jesus say to you?" Thomas said to them: "If I tell you one of the words he said to me, you will pick up stones and throw them at me, and fire will come out of the stones (and) burn you up." (The Gnostic Gospel of Thomas, Saying #13)[25]

This strange passage represents the type of secret knowledge that the Gnostic Jesus supposedly imparted to his disciples when he thought they were ready for it. In many ways this example is not unlike the mantras handed out to the followers of Hindu gurus who have reached a certain level of so-called enlightenment. Hindu mantras, or secret words, like those given to Thomas in the saying above, are not meant to be shared with anyone else. It would be completely out of character for Jesus to behave in this manner. Jesus freely gave His wisdom to all who would listen and hoped that they in turn would pass on the lessons to others.

> Jesus says: "If the flesh came into being because of the spirit, it is a wonder. But if the spirit (came into being) because of the body, it is a wonder of wonders." Yet I marvel at how this great wealth has taken up residence in this poverty. (The Gnostic Gospel of Thomas, Saying #29)[26]

The basic Gnostic belief that the spirit is good and the body is evil is reinforced by this passage. Again, Jesus would never make a statement like this. Nor would He purposely mislead His disciples regarding the truth about the future resurrection and the coming kingdom, as Saying #51 below has Him doing:

> His disciples said to him: "When will the resurrection of the dead take place, and when will the new world come?" He said to them: "That (resurrection) which you are awaiting has (already) come, but you do not recognize it." (The Gnostic Gospel of Thomas, Saying #51)[27]

Gnostic adherents today readily admit that the real apostle Thomas did not have anything to do with this manuscript, even though his name misleadingly (some would say fraudulently) appears as author in the text's opening verse. In fact, one disturbing trend can be seen in the naming of many of these Gnostic texts after biblical figures—such as the Gospel of Peter, the Gospel of Philip, the Gospel of Mary Magdalene, the Gospel of Bartholomew, the Apocryphon of John, and the Apocryphon of James—in order to give them an air of legitimacy.[28] There is no doubt that early Gnostic promoters attempted to gain credibility for their questionable documents by equating them with the writings of the apostles.

Rewriting History

Many of today's scholars who are in the business of promoting Gnosticism to the masses would do well to heed the apostle Paul's warning to the Corinthians that knowledge or *gnosis* has a tendency to lead to arrogance if not kept in check (1 Corinthians 8:2). Back in 1947, Danish historian M. P. Nilsson wrote about this very problem among those wishing to revive the beliefs of ancient Gnosticism. Those obsessed with promoting these theories, he said, seemed perfectly comfortable dismissing thousands of years of previous historical work and effort without the slightest hesitation—and replacing it with their own unsubstantiated views:

> These young scholars would imply that, in light of more recent research, the work of an older generation is fit only for the waste paper basket, but this is not true.[29]

Today's leading proponents of Gnosticism, including Elaine Pagels, freely admit that "new ways of thinking about Gnosticism" should be held in higher esteem and therefore take precedence over the historical data.[30]I can't help but ask the obvious … Why?

A notable attempt to rewrite history occurred in 1934 when German theologian Walter Bauer wrote a book called *Orthodoxy and Heresy in Earliest Christianity* that called into question the manner in which Christianity had been defined during the first four centuries following the birth of Jesus. At its core was the suggestion that what we regard today as Christian orthodoxy emerged victoriously, not because of the value of the evidence, but because of *favorable circumstances*. Bauer's book has since become the "bible" of modern-day Gnostic revivalists.

> If we follow such procedure and simply agree with the judgment of the anti-heretical fathers for the post New Testament period, do we all too quickly become dependent on the vote of but one party—that party which perhaps as much through favorable circumstances as by its own merit eventually was thrust into the foreground, and which possibly has at its disposal today the more powerful and thus the more prevalent voice—only because the chorus of others has been muted?[31]

What Bauer could not have foreseen was the discovery of the Nag Hammadi manuscripts a decade after the publication of his book. Combined together, these two elements became the catalyst for today's modern Gnostic revival.

In addition to various media outlets, the places that have witnessed the highest concentration of Gnostic proselytizing of the uninitiated have been college and university campuses. Most troubling has been the "gnostification" of young adults via courses that claim to offer instruction in the Bible itself. For example, at Harvard University, Helmut

Koester, professor of New Testament studies, has been championing the theories of Walter Bauer to his unsuspecting students for many, many years:

> Walter Bauer ... demonstrated convincingly in a brilliant monograph of 1934 that Christian groups labeled heretical actually predominated in the first two or three centuries, both geographically and theologically. Recent discoveries, especially those at Nag Hammadi in Upper Egypt, have made it even clearer that Bauer was essentially right and that a thorough and extensive re-evaluation of early Christian history is called for.[32]

Not all scholars have been so quick to endorse Bauer's work. In fact, many have found his pro-Gnostic arguments to be based on a complete lack of evidence. Fellow German historian Hans-Dietrich Altendorf didn't pull any punches when he classified Bauer's book as "constructive fantasy" and "elegantly worked-out fiction."[33] Likewise, Simone Pétrement, in her five-hundred-page volume *A Separate God*, meticulously details how it is impossible to demonstrate from the historical record that Gnosticism either came before, or existed alongside of, orthodox Christianity.[34] It can, however, be shown that Gnosticism came afterward as a *reaction or rebuttal* to it.

Those who view Bauer's work as successfully providing the starting point for today's Gnostic revival do so because it articulates the arguments they *want* to hear. It caters to the desires of a rebellious heart rather than presenting logically sound evidence for a Gnostic worldview.

The Gnostic God

Those wishing to get a handle on Gnostic theology are going to find they have their work cut out for them. Ancient Gnostic manuscripts are a study in contradiction. Some hold to a monotheistic (single) view of god while others project a polytheistic (multiple gods) perspective.

Despite being written over a period of fifteen hundred years by forty different authors, the sixty-six books that make up the Bible have a uniformly consistent view of God, His creation, and His relationship to man. Of course, no such common thread exists among Gnostic documents.

The Gnostic Gospel of Philip was among those texts found at the Nag Hammadi site and has been dated to the latter part of the second century or early third century. Once again, borrowed passages from the New Testament have been reinterpreted in order to give them a Gnostic thrust. Like the Gospel of Thomas, the Gospel of Philip is not really a gospel at all, but a haphazard collection of philosophical musings, although this time, only a handful of these statements have been attributed to Jesus.

The Gnostic belief that *knowledge* holds the key to salvation (as opposed to the work Jesus did on the cross) is presented in the Gospel of Philip along with the idea that truth comes from *within* each person (rather than from God). These two mystical principles form the foundation for not only Gnosticism, but for many of the alternative religions found throughout history.

> Ignorance is the mother of all evil. Ignorance will result
> in death, because those who come from ignorance
> neither were, nor are, nor shall be.... The Word said,
> "If you know the truth, the truth will make you free"

(John 8:32). Ignorance is a slave. Knowledge is freedom. If we know the truth, we shall find the fruits of
the truth within us. (The Gnostic Gospel of Philip)[35]

Both of these Gnostic concepts (that knowledge leads to eternal
life and that truth can be found within) are diametrically opposed
to the biblical precepts that state that salvation comes only through
Jesus Christ and that wickedness, not truth, resides within the human
heart:

> Nor is there salvation in any other, for there is no other
> name [besides Jesus Christ] under heaven given among
> men by which we must be saved. (Acts 4:12)

> For from within, out of the heart of men, proceed evil
> thoughts, adulteries, fornications, murders, thefts,
> covetousness, wickedness, deceit, lewdness, an evil
> eye, blasphemy, pride, foolishness. All these evil things
> come from within and defile a man. (Mark 7:21–23)

In addition, the Gospel of Philip's description of god and creation
can seem rather shocking to those who are used to hearing about such
things only from a Judeo-Christian perspective:

> The world came about through a mistake. For he
> who created it wanted to create it imperishable and
> immortal. He fell short of attaining his desire. For the
> world never was imperishable, nor, for that matter,
> was he who made the world. (The Gnostic Gospel of
> Philip)[36]

By claiming that the creation was a mistake, that the creator had limitations, and that god is not eternal, we once again find the Gnostic opinion challenging the very essence of the Bible at every stage:

> Then God saw everything that He had made, and indeed it was very good. (Genesis 1:31)

> Ah, Lord GOD! Behold, You have made the heavens and the earth by Your great power and outstretched arm. There is nothing too hard for You. (Jeremiah 32:17)

> Now to the King eternal, immortal, invisible, to God who alone is wise, be honor and glory forever and ever. (1 Timothy 1:17)

So Moses Got It Wrong?

Perhaps the most complete description of the character of the Gnostic god appears in the Apocryphon of John. This text also dates to the mid to late second century and is yet another of the many manuscripts found at Nag Hammadi. It purports to be a dialogue between the apostle John and Jesus, yet the information it contains is so far removed from any biblical documents that it can only be classified as mythological. In fact, the description of the manner in which the creation is carried by the various levels of gods and goddesses, complete with jealous infighting among the gods, is more akin to the polytheistic pagan beliefs of the surrounding Greco-Roman culture than anything else.

Throughout the document, the Gnostic Jesus continually explains to

John that Moses made numerous errors when writing the book of Genesis and then proceeds to provide the "correct" details regarding the nature of god and creation. According to this rather complex Gnostic text, the first act of god was to create a "virginal spirit" known as Barbelo:

> This is the first power which was before all of them and which came forth from his mind. She is the forethought of the All—her light shines like his light—the perfect power which is the image of the invisible, virginal Spirit who is perfect. The first power, the glory of Barbelo, the perfect glory in the aeons, the glory of the revelation, she glorified the virginal Spirit and it was she who praised him, because thanks to him she had come forth. This is the first thought, his image; she became the womb of everything, for it is she who is prior to them all, the Mother-Father. (The Gnostic Apocryphon of John)[37]

The next stage involved the creation of a series of lights and "aeons." Among these was a female god with an independent spirit named Sophia. This god, who would become our creator's creator, went ahead with an act of creation without the knowledge or consent of the primary god:

> And the Sophia of the Epinoia, being an aeon, conceived a thought from herself and the conception of the invisible Spirit and foreknowledge. She wanted to bring forth a likeness out of herself without the consent of the Spirit—he had not approved.... And because of the invincible power which is in her, her thought did not remain idle, and something came out of her which was imperfect and different from her appearance, because she

had created it without her consort. And it was dissimilar
to the likeness of its mother, for it has another form. (The
Gnostic Apocryphon of John)[38]

This secret creative act resulted in the formation of the first of the
"archons"—a lion-faced serpent named Yaltabaoth who introduced evil
into the world. Yaltabaoth would go on to create the first man and breathe
power into him.[39] Thus, according to the Apocryphon of John, which is
the most fully realized of all Gnostic texts, we humans were created by an
evil serpent who himself was mistakenly created by a female god, the result
of an act of rebellion!

Such a fanciful tale would normally be seen as an entertaining piece
of mythological literature were it not for the fact that *Jesus is supposed
to be the one who is presenting it as absolute truth!* Keep in mind that
each time you see a picture of Jesus emblazoned on the cover of the latest edition of *Time* or *Newsweek* magazine extolling the virtues of some
new "Christian" discovery or piece of information, the core belief of
Gnosticism as recounted above is likely to be the foundational theology
being promoted, whether it's mentioned in the article or not.

The Gnostic Jesus

The Gnostic view of Jesus varies from manuscript to manuscript. At times
he is portrayed as human with divine attributes as in the Gospel of Thomas
while at other times his divinity is so powerful that it overshadows any
human characteristics, such as in the Gnostic Gospel of the Egyptians. At
no time, however, is he portrayed as being merely human in any foundational Gnostic manuscript.

For example, in the Apocalypse of Peter, a ghostly yet happy Jesus appears to the apostle Peter floating above the cross while the less important physical Jesus is simultaneously being crucified. Peter asks:

> "Who is this one above the cross, who is glad and laughing? And is it another person whose feet and hands they are hammering?" The Savior said to me, "He whom you see above the cross, glad and laughing, is the living Jesus. But he into whose hands and feet they are driving the nails is the physical part, which is the substitute. They are putting to shame that which is his likeness." (The Gnostic Apocalypse of Peter)[40]

Similarly, in the Apocryphon of John, a ghostlike Gnostic Jesus appears before a tongue-tied apostle John and begins altering his physical appearance before revealing his role as a male-female deity:

> Behold, the heavens opened and the whole creation which is below heaven shone, and the world was shaken. I was afraid, and behold I saw in the light a youth who stood by me. While I looked at him, he became like an old man. And he changed his likeness (again), becoming like a servant. There was not a plurality before me, but there was a likeness with multiple forms in the light, and the likenesses appeared through each other, and the likeness had three forms. He said to me, "John, John, why do you doubt, or why are you afraid? You are not unfamiliar with this image, are you? That is, do not be timid! I am the one who is with you always. I am the Father, I am the Mother, I am the Son. I am the undefiled and incorruptible one." (The Gnostic Apocryphon of John)[41]

In another manuscript known as the Sophia of Jesus Christ, the Gnostic Jesus presented here has become so godlike as to have no need for a human form:

> From now on, I am the Great Savior. For he is immortal and eternal. Now he is eternal, having no birth; for everyone who has birth will perish. He is unbegotten, having no beginning; for everyone who has a beginning has an end. Since no one rules over him, he has no name; for whoever has a name is the creation of another. He is unnamable. He has no human form; for whoever has human form is the creation of another. (The Gnostic Sophia of Jesus Christ)[42]

By contrast, the New Testament writers, who were contemporaries of Jesus, clearly identified Him as someone who was both human and divine ... and they did it repeatedly and (unlike Gnostic texts) without contradiction:

> Jesus Christ our Lord, who was born of the seed of David according to the flesh, and declared to be the Son of God with power according to the Spirit of holiness, by the resurrection from the dead. (Romans 1:3–4)

A Gnostic Buffet

Even though every single foundational Gnostic text depicts Jesus as being at least partially if not fully divine, all of today's leading Gnostics portray

Jesus as being strictly human, without a shred of divinity. How can this be? The Jesus featured in Dan Brown's *The Da Vinci Code*, for example, is simply a mortal like everyone else who eventually married and had children. In James Tabor's *The Jesus Dynasty*, Jesus is a royal descendant of King David, but still merely human. In Michael Baigent's *The Jesus Papers*, Jesus remained human even after being "proclaimed God" by Emperor Constantine during the convening of the Council of Nicaea in the fourth century.[43] What's going on?

Likewise, since today's Gnostics have gone to such great lengths to deny the resurrection ever occurred, their own texts certainly must deny it as well, right? Well ... as a matter of fact, the Gnostic Gospel of Mary Magdalene purports to document an extended dialogue between Mary and the *resurrected* Jesus. In a similar vein, the Apocryphon of John is supposed to detail a "corrected" version of the creation story as recounted by a *risen* Jesus to the apostle John. Why would these folks go to such great lengths to validate the authenticity of these manuscripts and then dismiss what they have to say?

What is being promoted in our culture today is a type of *Gnostic buffet* where customers can simply pick and choose to believe whatever they want, *as long as it's not biblical Christianity*. It's almost as if the data is irrelevant. This has been the goal of Gnosticism for the last nineteen hundred years—*to undermine orthodox Christianity at any cost*. If the Gnostics must ignore portions of their own manuscripts; if they must create new information out of thin air; if they must change the manner in which ancient documents are dated in order to provide their manuscripts with preferably earlier dates; or if the entire historical record for the last two thousand years must be rewritten so that it can be shown that orthodox Christianity got it wrong, well then ... so be it!

Return to the Garden

The battle over Gnosticism being fought today was already fought eighteen centuries ago … with the same information, the same desire to derail orthodox Christianity, and the same lack of evidence to support the Gnostic perspective. The relatively new discoveries of Nag Hammadi are promoted as if they are "new" when in fact these same manuscripts have been around for eighteen hundred years. Likewise, the latest "secret" or "hidden" revelations detailed in recent newsmagazines or TV specials are in fact neither secret nor hidden. The apostle John dealt with the spirit behind such theories in his New Testament writings during the first century, while apologists such as Irenaeus dealt with the errors of the actual Gnostic manuscripts themselves throughout the second. The difference today is that the Gnostics have the educational systems and global media on their side.

One of the more recent attacks on Christianity and the character of Christ has come from veteran Dutch filmmaker and Jesus Seminar member Paul Verhoeven through his book *Jesus of Nazareth: A Realistic Portrait*. In it he claims that Jesus was the resulting product of a sexual union between Mary and a Roman soldier who raped her:

> The 69-year-old director, who also directed "Showgirls"—starring Elizabeth Berkley in one of the most panned films of the '90's—and sci-fi action hits like "Total Recall" and "Robo-Cop," as well as the sci-fi bust "Starship Troopers," claims he and co-biographer Rob van Scheers have written the most realistic portrayal of Jesus ever published. In addition to suggesting that the Virgin Mary may have been a rape victim, the book will also say that Christ was not betrayed by Judas Iscariot, one of the 12 original apostles of Jesus, as the New Testament states….

Verhoeven hopes it will be a springboard for him to raise interest in making a film along the same lines.[44]

Why is it so important to these people that Jesus be portrayed as someone other than who He really is? Why must the resurrection of Christ be dispensed with? Why must His work on the cross be undermined? And why must *knowledge of evil* replace *Jesus* as our source of salvation?

In a way, *gnosis* is what got the human race into trouble in the first place. God has nothing against people having knowledge, but He simply did not wish to contaminate His creation with *evil*. When Adam and Eve, utilizing their free will, chose to rebel against their Creator, they did so not because they wanted to know the difference between good and evil, but because they wanted to know and experience *evil* itself. They already had a working knowledge of *good*:

> Then the serpent said to the woman, "You will not surely die. For God knows that in the day you eat of it [the fruit] your eyes will be opened, and you will be like God, knowing good and evil." (Genesis 3:4–5)

The Devil is identified right off the bat in the first book of the Old Testament as the source behind the knowledge of evil. In Gnosticism, this knowledge is what brings about salvation. Yet, the Gnostics have the audacity to take it a step further. Instead of acknowledging who the real source of evil is, they have replaced the role of the Devil in Gnosticism with Jesus! In the following excerpt from the Apocryphon of John, Jesus, who is narrating the story, is the one who convinces Adam and Eve to eat of the fruit that will lead to the knowledge of evil. Therefore, within Gnosticism, the wise, sagelike Gnostic Jesus, who is the giver of knowledge, becomes the Devil himself:

But what they call the tree of knowledge of good and
evil, which is the Epinoia of the light, they stayed in
front of it in order that he (Adam) might not look up to
his fullness and recognize the nakedness of his shameful-
ness. But it was I (Jesus) who brought about that they
ate. (The Gnostic Apocryphon of John)[45]

The Bible is clear about the reason behind the existence of evil and
death in our world, yet also provides the means by which we may overcome sin and death:

Therefore, just as through one man [Adam] sin entered
the world, and death through sin, and thus death spread
to all men, because all sinned. (Romans 5:12)

But God demonstrates His own love toward us, in that
while we were still sinners, Christ died for us. (Romans
5:8)

Whoever believes in Him [Jesus] should not perish but
have eternal life. (John 3:15)

Judas: Our Hero?

In the upside-down, topsy-turvy world of Gnosticism, it should come as
no surprise then that Judas Iscariot, the man who betrayed Jesus for thirty
pieces of silver and then hanged himself, is the true hero in all of this. On
April 9, 2006, National Geographic aired a television program promoting

the virtues of the newly discovered "lost" Gospel of Judas. Unearthed in a cave in Egypt in 1978, this document presents Judas as the greatest of all the disciples because he was the one who caused the death of Christ![46] It is Judas who helps the Gnostic Jesus rid himself of his evil earthly body, and for that he should be praised. Of course, the Gospel of Judas is not new. Eighteen hundred years prior to the National Geographic exposure, Irenaeus had already addressed this particular Gnostic creation in his work *Against Heresies:*

> They declare that Judas the traitor was thoroughly acquainted with these things, and that he alone, knowing the truth as no others did, accomplished the mystery of the betrayal; by him all things, both earthly and heavenly, were thus thrown into confusion. They produce a fictitious history of this kind, which they style the Gospel of Judas.[47]

Finally, there is noted author Bart Ehrman, the "former Christian" who now claims to be an agnostic. By choosing to weigh in on this document, he reveals his strong allegiance with Gnosticism as evidenced by his unapologetic and chilling promotion of his hero Judas—as he is portrayed in the Gospel of Judas:

> Judas was the only one of the disciples who understood his Lord. Jesus came not from the creator god but from the realm of Barbelo. So, too, did some of us. Some of us are trapped here in the prisons of our bodies, but once we learn the truth that Jesus delivered to his one faithful disciple, Judas, we will be able to escape to return to our heavenly home. Judas is the one who

leads the way…. Judas performed for him the greatest service imaginable. His betrayal was not the act of a traitor to the cause. It was a kind deed performed for the sake of his Lord. He turned Jesus over to the authorities so that Jesus could be killed and escape the confines of his body. In doing so, Judas is the greatest of all the apostles.[48]

So, according to the tenets of Gnosticism, if one wishes to rise to the level of greatness, or if one wishes to demonstrate how much they care for another person—be it Jesus or anyone else for that matter, they must arrange to have them killed!

Many false religions in existence today have their beginnings in Gnosticism. And it's very likely that the false messiahs, who will continue to increase in number as we enter the *last days*, will adopt and promote many of these same Gnostic ideas. In fact, those who cause their family members and friends to be put to death during the future tribulation period will be, in Bart Ehrman's own words, performing "the greatest service imaginable" and "a kind deed" by helping them "escape the confines of their bodies" (see Luke 21:16). The apostle Paul's warning to the Ephesian elders is just as relevant today as it was back then:

> For I know this, that after my departure savage wolves will come in among you, not sparing the flock. Also from among yourselves men will rise up, speaking perverse things, to draw away the disciples after themselves. Therefore watch, and remember that for three years I did not cease to warn everyone night and day with tears. (Acts 20:29–31)

A Heart's Desire

Ultimately, it comes down to what's inside each individual human heart. Even Gnostic expert Elaine Pagels is unable to hide the real reason behind her rejection of the Christian gospel, as evidenced here in this quotation from fellow mystic Michael Baigent:

> In an unusual move for an academic, Pagels, an expert on the Gnostic texts, introduces a personal note in her book *Beyond Belief: The Secret Gospel of Thomas*. The note addresses a crucial point with far-reaching consequences: what she cannot love in the Church, she explained, is "the tendency to identify Christianity with a single authorized set of beliefs ... coupled with the conviction that Christian belief alone offers access to God."[49]

It is this final statement ... that *Jesus alone offers access to God and heaven* that the Gnostics, skeptics, atheists, and humanists can't seem to handle. But it is what Jesus and the apostles taught, and what millions in the early church died defending:

> "Let not your heart be troubled; you believe in God, believe also in Me. In My Father's house are many mansions; if it were not so, I would have told you. I go to prepare a place for you. And if I go and prepare a place for you, I will come again and receive you to Myself; that where I am, there you may be also. And where I go you know, and the way you know." Thomas said to Him, "Lord, we do not know where You are going, and how can we know the way?" Jesus said to him, "I am the way,

the truth, and the life. No one comes to the Father except
through Me." (John 14:1–6)

According to Jesus, either He is the only way to God, or there is no
way. Who would you say is easier to believe … the enemies of Jesus who
distort His character, the modern-day Gnostics who base their faith on
discredited shadowy manuscripts, or Jesus Himself who demonstrated that
He was alive after the resurrection by "many infallible proofs"?

Chapter Nine

NOW AS ALWAYS, JESUS CHANGES LIVES

For I am not ashamed of the gospel of Christ, for it is the power of God to salvation for everyone who believes. (Romans 1:16)

There is no other person in the history of the world who has changed more lives for the better than Jesus Christ. The dramatic transformation experienced by Saul of Tarsus, one of the chief persecutors of the early church, is a classic example. Even today, the skeptics and antagonists of Christianity cannot seem to explain what happened to this man.

Then Saul, still breathing threats and murder against the disciples of the Lord, went to the high priest and asked letters from him to the synagogues of Damascus, so that if he found any who were of the Way, whether men or women, he might bring them bound to Jerusalem. As he journeyed he came near Damascus, and suddenly a

light shone around him from heaven. Then he fell to the
ground, and heard a voice saying to him, "Saul, Saul, why
are you persecuting Me?" And he said, "Who are You,
Lord?" Then the Lord said, "I am Jesus, whom you are
persecuting." (Acts 9:1–5)

When Saul encountered the resurrected Jesus on the Damascus Road,
his experience of salvation by faith in Christ was so extraordinary that
he changed from being the most vicious destroyer of Christians into the
greatest builder of the church the world has ever seen. Through Jesus, Saul
of Tarsus became Paul the apostle. Paul's subsequent life, New Testament
writings, missionary journeys, and ultimate imprisonment and martyrdom
for his faith demonstrated beyond a doubt just how far Christ's transforming power was able to work on someone so lost.

Undiminished Power

It is amazing to realize that the preceding two thousand years have not
diminished this transforming power of Jesus one iota. Millions of similar
life-changing experiences have occurred throughout the ages to those who
have simply believed and committed their lives to Him.

For the message of the cross is foolishness to those who
are perishing, but to us who are being saved it is the power
of God. (1 Corinthians 1:18)

As a pastor for thirty-seven of my sixty years of ministry, I can
testify to witnessing literally thousands of lives similarly transformed

before my eyes. In case after case I have watched as those immersed in debauchery and self-indulgence have miraculously changed into decent, law-abiding, and productive citizens. The following are just a few examples.

Deacon Chuck

During the 2007 Christmas holiday season, my wife and I visited the church in San Diego that we had previously pastored for twenty-five years. Chuck, a deacon and spiritual leader in that church for many years, met me in the foyer and thanked me for leading him to accept Christ back in 1974. Recognizing him, but forgetting what his profession was at the time, I asked, "Chuck, what were you when you accepted Jesus?" Quick as a flash he said, "I was a first-class heathen!" If you knew Chuck today you would have never imagined he could have been that kind of person. All it took was for someone to befriend him, to invite him to our church, and for him to receive Christ in order to make a difference in his life.

The Bookseller Giant

My reunion with Deacon Chuck reminded me of something that happened in July at the annual Christian booksellers convention in Atlanta. A giant of a man was waiting in line where Jerry Jenkins (my partner and coauthor of the Left Behind series) and I were autographing books. When he stepped up to the table I took one look at him and half-jokingly asked, "Who did you play football for?" Then I noticed tears in his eyes as he said, "I want to thank you guys for your books. They led me to Christ." Then he added, "Until my wife gave me your book to read, I was a first-class heathen. That was eleven years ago. Today I am here at this convention as the representative of a Christian publisher." Jerry looked at me and said, "It sounds like Satan lost another one." And he was right.

Thousands have contacted us, telling us their stories of coming to faith after reading our Left Behind series about what life will be like during the tribulation after the rapture of the church takes place. Many are excited to share with us their life-changing experience of committing themselves by faith to Jesus Christ.

Released from Prison

The waitress at the Applebee's restaurant took one look at me and asked, "Are you the minister who wrote *Left Behind*?" When I said "yes" she burst into tears and had to excuse herself for a few moments. I glanced over at my wife, Beverly, with a slightly puzzled expression. My wife then proceeded to break the awkwardness of the situation by reminding me that I often have that effect on women. Upon returning to take our order, the slightly more composed waitress told us how she had accepted Christ while in jail. It seems she had gotten hooked on drugs in her late teens, had sold her body into prostitution, and was finally apprehended while selling drugs and sent to prison.

Fortunately, the restaurant was practically empty because by this time she was weeping once again. Through her tears she told us she had spent three years in the penitentiary during which time her husband had divorced her and taken custody of their daughter. She went on to say that somehow she heard about our Left Behind series and signed up on the prison library waiting list for the book. Three months later she got ahold of it. After reading the book, she prayed to receive Christ while on her knees in her cell, just like the characters did in the story. By this time she was crying at our table uncontrollably and stated what I have heard so many others say throughout the years, "… and Jesus changed my life!"

NOW AS ALWAYS, JESUS CHANGES LIVES

Instead of continuing to be a problem prisoner, she immediately transformed into a model inmate and was released on probation several years early. Looking into her attractive face I found it hard to believe she had descended so far into sin, for it didn't show. She then went on to tell us how she became involved with a Bible-believing church and for the past two years had lived a victorious life. During our meal she came back to our table and asked us to pray that the court would return custody of her sixteen-year-old daughter to her. The hearing was two weeks away.

Two months later she saw us come into the restaurant again. She came up to us, gave us a warm hug, and told us how she had successfully received custody of her daughter. Not only that, she had enrolled in college and was planning to go into nursing so she could help others.

I have yet to find anyone who has been transformed in such a manner as a result of converting to atheism, humanism, Gnosticism, or any other alternative religion. Only the message of the cross has the power to change lives for the better.

A Difficult Addiction

Sexual addiction is one of the most powerful addictions, with homosexuality likely being the strongest of all. It is so difficult to see a permanent change in this type of addiction. The psychological association that once claimed homosexuality was a mental disorder has since changed its definition, and now classifies it as a normal alternative lifestyle.

I experienced a graphic example of this a while back when I was a guest on a Los Angeles radio talk show discussing this very subject with a secular psychiatrist. He made the bold assertion that it is impossible for a homosexual man to become a heterosexual. He became incredulous when I stated that during my twenty-five years as a pastor in San Diego I had seen at least thirty homosexuals accept Christ, become literally transformed by the message of the cross, and successfully become heterosexuals. At first he called me a liar live on the radio! Then he made this statement: "I have been a practicing psychiatrist in Los Angeles for thirty-three years and I have never seen a homosexual changed, nor do I know any other counselor in the LA basin who has." Naturally, he became further infuriated when I explained that it was because he was counseling without the message of the cross, which "is the power of God to salvation for everyone who believes."[1]

That night I spoke at a church and mentioned my encounter with the psychiatrist. After my talk, I noticed a rather shy couple with two small children, waiting to talk to me. He was holding their baby and she held the hand of their little girl. He said, "I appreciated your message tonight regarding Christ's ability to change the heart of homosexuals." As we shook hands he confessed, "We heard your debate with the psychiatrist on the radio. Now you can say you have met the thirty-first homosexual whose life was turned around by faith in Christ."

The next night I drove to Santa Barbara where I told that story during a message to another church gathering and had three more former homosexuals come up to me afterward and tell me their lives had been changed by accepting Jesus Christ as their Savior. I've since had many more tell me the same thing.

There is no question that there are literally thousands of ex-homosexuals today living regular lives, many with a wife and children, because of their belief in Jesus Christ. In fact, there is an organization called *Exit Ministries* in every state in America that is helping homosexuals to leave that lifestyle. Most of the directors are former homosexuals themselves. They delight in sharing the good news that there is a way out of this powerful addiction through faith in the risen Christ.

In case you think this transformation may not last, let me tell you about one of the long-term deacons in our church in San Diego. He was one of the first homosexuals I saw transformed by faith in Christ. That was over forty years ago. He didn't just come out of that lifestyle; he became an avid Bible reader and active member of our church, which is where he eventually met the girl of his dreams. I had the privilege of marrying them. They have since raised three Christian children and have lived a long and happy life. No one but Jesus Christ can transform people like that.

A word of caution is important here. Every homosexual I have encountered has been a heavy user of pornography. Originally it was via the printed page, then video, and now the Internet. Here is the point: No one can overcome sexual sins and continue viewing pornography.

Years ago I helped a man in the ministry leave that lifestyle by encouraging him to surrender his life to Christ. He lived a victorious life for years and eventually returned to the ministry. But then he fell back into homosexuality. I immediately asked if he had resumed looking at pornography and he said yes. Only by repenting of the addiction to pornography could he finally overcome the attraction of same-sex addiction. Which makes sense, for the Bible says, "As [a man] thinks in his heart so is he" (Proverbs 23:7). The eyes are a vehicle to the mind, and the mind is a direct path to our emotional center, the heart.

> For the weapons of our warfare are not carnal but mighty
> in God for pulling down strongholds, casting down argu-
> ments and every high thing that exalts itself against the
> knowledge of God, bringing every thought into captivity
> to the obedience of Christ. (2 Corinthians 10:4–5)

Not all of the homosexuals I have seen come to faith in Christ have been instantly or permanently cured. It usually takes three to six months to eradicate from their minds those images that have been burned into their imaginations, which in turn inflame their emotional passions. Only through total abstinence from viewing and thinking about such materials will these men eventually be able to find freedom from this life-shortening sin (the average life span of a homosexual man is at least twenty years less than that of the general population).[2]

Antisocial

At a deacons' meeting one night we were all shocked to hear one of our best church leaders say, "I'm a recovered alcoholic!" He went on to explain that he had come to faith in Christ eighteen years before and his life had dramatically changed. No longer did he come in at all hours of the night and disrupt his household. His growing love for Christ had increased his love for his family and, conversely, his family's love for him. For eighteen years he had completely stayed away from alcohol.

Our respected Christian brother went on to say that he was among the 10 percent of the population that have a built-in chemical affinity toward alcohol that they can't control. One shot of any type of alcohol and they immediately lose control. Having Christ in one's life does not enable such a person to become a social drinker. But Jesus can give this type of person victory over the obsession to take that first drink.

We had a man accept Christ in our church who had spent three years in prison for committing an alcohol-induced robbery. He managed to stay sober for six years. One hot day while at the car dealership where he was employed he thought to himself, "A cold glass of beer would sure taste good right now." Rather than change his thinking to "I am a recovering alcoholic," he began to focus his thoughts on how refreshing it would be and said to himself, "It's been six years since I've had any, I think I can control it now." Within two months he had not only lost that control, but his family, his job, his Christian testimony, and his freedom.

When he finally got out of prison this time he was left with nothing.

His wife did not love him, his three sons did not respect him, and he was unemployable. It took several years for him to finally learn to trust God for victory over his addiction and remain a recovering alcoholic for the rest of his life. Had he learned that lesson a few years earlier, he would have been able to hold on to what he had.

The Coffee Shop

In the early 1980s, my wife and I had a weekly TV program called *Family Life*. One of our early guests was a forty-year-old former prostitute who had sold her body in order to buy drugs. She claimed she had had sex with "at least five thousand men."

One day while in a coffee shop she met a man "who was different. He treated me with respect and politeness," she said. It wasn't long until they were having lunch together on a regular basis. She offered to have sex with him "for free" because he was "so nice" to her. He refused and told her that he too had been "a great sinner." A friend had led him to accept Jesus Christ. In time she too accepted this Savior named Jesus and turned her back on that lifestyle. The couple was later married. When we met them, they didn't look like people who had lived such degrading lives. By then they had started a ministry to all types of addicts, offering them hope for salvation and a transformation of life.

Two thousand years after His death for our sins, followed by His resurrection and subsequent ascension into heaven, Jesus is still transforming those who call upon Him by faith.

The Transformation of John Newton

Nearly everyone has heard of the Reverend John Newton, who wrote what is often referred to as America's favorite hymn, "Amazing Grace."

Few realized until they saw the movie with the same name released in 2006 that John Newton had been a slave trader for many years. He admitted transporting twenty thousand African slaves to the New World, many of whom died in transit. Finally the screams and tears of the slaves got to his conscience and he realized that he was a great sinner who was in need of a great Savior. During a violent storm at sea in 1747, he became so terrified that he prayed that the Lord would save him and his ship's cargo, and soon afterward, received "that great Savior" as his own.

Newton eventually became a pastor and led a gentleman by the name of William Wilberforce to faith in Christ. He encouraged Wilberforce to remain in the British Parliament where he could be in a position to help abolish England's slave trade.

It has been my observation that a truly repentant person doesn't project himself as "a good person" but instead as "a sinner." Perhaps that is why the song "Amazing Grace" is so popular among sincere believers:

> Amazing Grace, how sweet the sound
> That saved a wretch like me.
> I once was lost but now am found,
> Was blind, but now I see.

The Redeemed Sinner Showdown

My longtime friend, the late Dr. D. James Kennedy, in his book *What If Jesus Had Never Been Born?* wrote about a man named Charles Bradlaugh, a nineteenth-century atheist who challenged Hugh Price Hughes, an active Christian evangelist working among the poor in the slums of London, to a debate on the validity of Christianity. Hughes told Bradlaugh he would agree to the debate on one condition: He said, "I propose to you that we each bring some concrete evidences of the validity of our beliefs in the form of men and women who have been redeemed from the lives of sin and shame by the influence of our teaching. I will bring one hundred such men and women, and I challenge you to do the same."

Hughes then said that if Bradlaugh couldn't bring one hundred, then he could bring fifty; if he couldn't bring fifty, then he could bring twenty. He finally whittled the number down to one. All Bradlaugh had to do was to find one person whose life was improved by atheism and Hughes—who would bring one hundred people improved by Christ—would agree to debate him. Bradlaugh eventually withdrew.[3]

The Recidivism Rate

During the Nixon administration a very special attorney in our church was flown back to the White House to be interviewed by the president and his staff. They were considering him for the position of commissioner of the IRS. He was well qualified, for in addition to having won the largest case ever against the IRS for defending an Imperial Valley farmer, he had been a CPA prior to going to law school. However, he returned to San Diego a very disillusioned man. The special legal counsel to the president, a man by the name of Chuck Colson, had given this attorney the impression that Colson was "a very evil man." In fact, I remember his very words to this day when he said, "Of all the evil people in the world I have ever met, Colson is the last person I would like to have back me up in a meeting." Therefore, I was not surprised when President Nixon fell into disgrace as a result of the Watergate cover-up, and Colson was identified as "Nixon's hatchet man." Chuck Colson would eventually spend nine months in federal prison.

A close associate to Colson, Jeb Magruder, who served Nixon as the deputy director of the Committee to Re-elect the President, had this to say about Colson in 1974:

I came to regard Colson as an evil genius. His brilliance was undeniable, but it was too often applied to encouraging Richard Nixon's darker side—his desire to lash out at his enemies, his instinct for the jugular. I would have to say—granting Nixon's central responsibility for what happened in his administration—Colson was one of the men among his advisers most responsible for creating the climate that made Watergate possible, perhaps inevitable.[4]

What makes Chuck Colson's story so amazing and serves as a great illustration of the type of change Jesus can make in a person's life, is the manner in which he has lived since his conversion to Christ while in prison. Chuck tells his amazing story in his book *Born Again*. My friend, the late pastor D. James Kennedy tells how God changed this political bigwig-turned-felon:

> Today, this very same Chuck Colson heads a ministry he started that preaches the gospel to tens of thousands of inmates. Prison Fellowship, which grew out of Colson's own jailhouse experience, is now a worldwide outreach located in northern Virginia that helped more than 100,000 prisoners last year. It ministers to them in prison and helps them get readjusted once they're out of prison and back into society. Prison Fellowship even provides Christmas gifts for the families of inmates. Many people today also know Colson for his magnificent books, his inspiring talks, and his daily radio commentary, *Break Point with Chuck Colson*. Colson's genius refreshes people every day worldwide. Take Christ out of the equation and all we're left with is an evil genius.[5]

The "born again" experience that changed Colson's life and launched a prison fellowship ministry more than thirty years ago has changed thousands of lives. The proof lies in the amazing drop in the recidivism rate (criminals who return to prison after they've been released) of those who have received Jesus' life-changing message. It is a known fact that 75 percent of all violent prisoners are reincarcerated within three years—with the exception of those who were converted in prison and discipled in the Word of God. For these inmates, the recidivism rate drops to 24 percent.

Think of it, thousands of men and women have returned to their homes and families, found employment, and have become good citizens. Are they perfect? No, they are still human and have a lot of changes to make. But their commitment to Jesus Christ gives them a new lease on life. Jesus not only changes lives, He does it consistently.

Quoth the Raven

While a friend named Rob in Southern California was serving as a youth pastor, he had a strange encounter with a mother and daughter who had come in for counseling. The mother was an affluently dressed business-woman talking constantly on her cell phone. Her fourteen-year-old daughter, Raven, was simply "out of control." She was dressed in black from top to bottom and spewing forth the most vicious profanities he had heard in a long time. Her mother spoke up: "I don't think seeing a minister will do any good, but we've tried psychiatrists and doctors and nothing seems to work. She is scheduled to check into a psych ward this week. This is just a last resort." Pastor Rob explained to Raven that she would just be given more medication, continue to hear more voices in her head, and sink deeper into despair in the psych ward. However, if she would just call out to God, ask Him for help, and pledge to serve

Him, He would help her. His closing prayer was met with more cursing and blasphemies from this seemingly demon-possessed young girl.

Two years later Rob took 150 youth group members to a mountain camp where over five hundred teens gathered and were met with an incredible outpouring of the Holy Spirit. Many came to faith in Christ and numerous others recommitted themselves to serve God. A girl named Savannah wept for joy as she watched God at work in the lives of these young people, particularly among those she had invited to the camp. She had even paid the way out of her own pocket for several friends to attend.

Rob watched as Savannah started to approach him. But he was not prepared for her question. "Pastor Rob, do you remember me?" He said, "No, I'm sorry." She replied, "When we first met I told you my name was Raven." Rob could not believe his eyes! Savannah continued, "When I was Raven, I was sent to the hospital. The doctors gave me more and more medication until I would sit on the floor with my knees drawn up under my chin, rocking back and forth for hours. I heard all kinds of voices in my head, screaming at me, and they wouldn't stop. I thought I was going mad. Finally, I remembered what you had said. I called out to God saying, 'If You can hear me, please help me, and I will spend the rest of my life serving You.' And He did! For over a year now I have been a different person. I accepted Christ and He changed my life!" The new youth pastor who had brought her over to Pastor Rob told him, "Savannah is one of the best leaders in our youth group."

Only Jesus changes lives like that consistently.

> All that the Father gives Me will come to Me, and the one who comes to Me I will by no means cast out. (John 6:37)

Sarah's Throwaway Girls

During his first term in office, President Ronald Reagan gave a speech in Orlando, Florida. On his flight back to Washington he read about Sarah Trollinger's home for "throwaway" girls in the local Orlando paper. He was moved by the account of this Christian woman who had started a life-changing home for teenage girls who had fallen into drugs, prostitution, and other vices. No one wanted them, not even their parents. Local judges were so impressed with the dramatic results Sarah was having, they would constantly call and ask, "Can you take another girl? I don't want to put her in jail—the hardened criminals would destroy her, and if I put her in juvenile hall, she would destroy them."

Sarah's home touched President Reagan so much that he personally wrote out a check to her ministry for one thousand dollars and had it mailed to her when they touched down in Washington. I actually saw a copy of his personal check framed on the wall in Sarah's home for girls.

The next time I saw the girls was when Sarah brought about twenty of them to my wife's Concerned Women for America convention in the nation's capital to tell their story. Listening to these lovely girls speak about how Jesus "changed their lives" was an amazing experience! I could not imagine their terrible situations prior to Jesus coming into their hearts, seeing how happy they were now. They were shining trophies of His marvelous saving grace! This faith-based ministry continues to save hundreds of girls from a lifetime of suffering, heartache, and in many cases premature sickness and death—not to mention saving millions of dollars in law-enforcement costs for the people of Orlando.

Recently Beverly and I were invited back to Orlando to speak to a group of a thousand pastors and their wives, after which Sarah came up to greet us. What a reunion. Twenty years had passed. Sarah told us that she had started a school for boys as well as a program that trained other women to start similar life-changing programs in their own cities. Currently, they have sixty-eight such schools around the country.

These incredible stories barely scratch the surface of the untold millions of similar accounts happening around the world on a daily basis. Of course, the common denominator in all of these transformations is Jesus Christ.

> Therefore, if anyone is in Christ, he is a new creation; old things have passed away; behold, all things have become new. (2 Corinthians 5:17)

Chapter Ten

WHO DO YOU SAY I AM?

There is a hill in Israel known as Mount Megiddo. It is made up of more than two dozen layers of ruins from ancient cities that were built atop one another during the preceding millenniums. If you were to stand on this mount today, you could gaze out over the magnificent Megiddo Valley below. This flat expanse of land that runs for miles in three directions is truly a breathtaking sight. During his first visit to the area, Napoleon Bonaparte is rumored to have remarked that he thought the valley would be perfect for use as a battlefield.[1]

This area, in fact, served as the location for the first documented battle in recorded history, which occurred between the armies of the Egyptian pharaoh Thutmose III and a coalition of Canaanites in 1478 BC.[2] Ironically, the Valley of Megiddo is also scheduled to be the site of the final and greatest war the world will ever experience—the battle of Armageddon.[3]

As the unprecedented horrors of the seven-year tribulation period come to a climax, the armies of the world will launch what will most likely be an all-out nuclear exchange against Israel under the direction of the Antichrist at this site. The death toll and level of destruction will be unimaginable. Only through the direct intervention of the resurrected Jesus returning to earth at the height of this battle will mankind be prevented from destroying itself.[4] At that point, Christ will set up His millennial kingdom and rule over a peace-filled world for a thousand years,[5] in fulfill-ment of biblical prophecy.

Hold the Mao

Today, the Megiddo Valley appears serene and peaceful and sits in stark contrast to both its turbulent past and prophesied future. Now imagine for a moment the world's aggregate population gathered from throughout his-tory standing side by side in this enormous, beautiful valley. Of the more than thirteen billion people assembled here, which one person would be selected as having had the most influence on the world? Aristotle? Sir Isaac Newton? George Washington? Karl Marx? Mao Tse-tung?

Throughout this book we've shown how Jesus Christ impacted the world more than anyone who has ever lived. Without question He is in a category all by Himself. Remember, He was a thirty-year-old carpenter from an obscure town called Nazareth who hung up His tools and began a teaching ministry that lasted only three and a half years. Yet He was able to ultimately influence billions of lives. No one has done that before or since.

While on earth, Jesus predicted that He would return a second time. And while we don't know exactly when that will be, we do know that we are one day closer to it than we were yesterday. In fact, the second coming of Christ is three times as certain as His first appearance since there are three times as many recorded prophecies predicting His second coming (more than three hundred) compared to those foretell-ing His first.

The Big Lie

When I joined the ministry over a half century ago, the big lie taught at the time by liberal theologians was that "Jesus never claimed He was God." I don't know which New Testament written by what apostles they were reading, but it certainly wasn't the one I was preaching from three times a week. Nor was it the one I have based all of my books upon. With time, I have come to realize that many of them were trying to purposely disparage the virgin birth of Jesus, His sinless life, His sacrificial death, and His bodily resurrection—the very facts for which martyrs throughout the ages have given up their lives defending.

During His conversation with the woman at the well, Jesus made it abundantly clear who He was:

> The woman said to Him, "I know that Messiah is coming"
> (who is called Christ). "When He comes, He will tell us
> all things." Jesus said to her, "*I* who speak to you *am* He."
> (John 4:25–26)

In this passage, Jesus used the sacred name of God (I Am) to describe Himself—the same name God had given to Moses to describe Himself in Exodus 3:13–14, which means "the uncaused cause" (eternal creator) or "the source" of all things. John, in the introduction to his gospel, illuminated things even more by attributing the creation as we know it to Jesus prior to His coming to the earth.

> He was in the beginning with God. All things were made
> through Him, and without Him nothing was made that
> was made. (John 1:2–3)

Jesus was not reluctant to use the name "I Am" in reference to Himself—a name so sacred to the Jews of His day that they would not even utter it aloud. Consider the following self-identifiers Jesus used that were recorded by John in his gospel:

"I am the bread of life" (John 6:35, 41, 48, 51)

"I am the light of the world" (John 8:12)

"I am the door" (John 10:7, 9)

"I am the good shepherd" (John 10:11, 14)

"I am the resurrection and the life" (John 11:25)

"I am the way, the truth, and the life" (John 14:6)

"I am the true vine" (John 15:1, 5)

Jesus knew who He was and why He came to this earth. And He did not hide it from His first-century followers or the billions who have followed Him since. Speaking in the temple before a group of angry religious leaders, Jesus made it abundantly clear who He really was:

I and My Father are one. (John 10:30)

The Last Hope

Even after two thousand years, Jesus remains the ultimate changer of lives. No one has cured more addictions, restored more broken marriages, or repaired more effects from damaged childhoods than this former carpenter from Nazareth. You could say He is the *last* hope for those who have *lost* hope.

Still, Jesus Christ continues to be universally hated by the atheists, liberals, and skeptics of the world who are obsessed with trying to destroy people's faith. The question is why? The eighteenth-century French philosopher Voltaire spent most of his life attempting to undermine Christianity and yet ended up calling out to Jesus on his deathbed.[6] Simply put, atheism is not a very good philosophy to live by and an even worse one to die by.

The amazing transformation of lives continues despite never-ending misinformation campaigns about Jesus Christ in the liberal media and in many of this country's institutes of higher education. But even with such destructive obstacles, we still have it better in the United States than in most other countries (at least for now). Today, we find various authoritarian governments around the world continuing to force their Christian citizens to keep their beliefs hidden or else face execution. Those living under such repressive regimes look upon the religious freedoms we have in this country with envy. Rather than taking these freedoms for granted, we in America should instead be grateful for the long-range insight and sacrifices made on our behalf by our founding fathers.

America Does a 180

Of the fifty-five men who attended the original Constitutional Convention in Philadelphia in 1787, fifty-three were members of Protestant denominations while the other two were Catholic.[7] Most of them shared a deep love and respect for Jesus Christ. Many today fail to realize that the secret to our nation's greatness is a direct result of the fact that America was founded upon biblical principles.

Upon his death in 1638, the Reverend John Harvard bequeathed half of his estate along with his entire library consisting of four hundred Christian books and Bibles brought over from England to a fledgling Massachusetts university named in his honor.[8] For the next three centuries, the prestigious Harvard University, America's oldest institute of higher learning, would provide its students with an unsurpassed level of biblically based education.

Having such an inspiring foundation makes Harvard's conversion into the anti-Christian, pro-Gnostic vehicle that it is today all the more heartbreaking. As an illustration, consider this ... by 2005, the university had launched a multimillion-dollar research project designed to prove that God had absolutely nothing to do with the creation of life, as confirmed by Harvard professor of chemistry and chemical biology, Dr. David Liu:

> My expectation is that we will be able to reduce this [the creation of life] to a very simple series of logical events that could have taken place with no divine intervention.[9]

With many public school teachers and the majority of college and university professors espousing similar views to those of Dr. Liu, most students over the past fifty years who have submitted to America's educational system have been kept in the dark regarding our country's biblical foundation and Christian heritage. Such a wholesale withholding of information has no doubt contributed to the ongoing secularization (and subsequent moral decline) of our culture. There's a reason why the United

States became such a great nation in such an amazingly short amount of time, and it had everything to do with the prudence of our nation's founding fathers and their commitment to Jesus Christ. Consider the following:

> The Christian religion is, above all the religions that ever prevailed or existed in ancient or modern times, the religion of wisdom, virtue, equity, and humanity. (John Adams, second president of the United States; signer of the Declaration of Independence and the Bill of Rights)[10]

> The birthday of the nation is indissolubly linked with the birth of the Savior. The Declaration of Independence laid the cornerstone of human government upon the first precepts of Christianity. (John Quincy Adams, sixth president of the United States; secretary of state; U.S. senator)[11]

> I do not believe that the Constitution was the offspring of inspiration, but I am as satisfied that it is as much the work of Divine Providence as any of the miracles recorded in the Old and New Testaments. (Benjamin Rush, signer of the Declaration of Independence)[12]

> We pray that universal happiness may be established in the world, that all may bow to the scepter of our Lord Jesus Christ, and the whole earth be filled with His glory. (John Hancock, signer of the Declaration of Independence; president of Continental Congress)[13]

Without the almighty power of the Spirit of God enlight-
ening your mind, subduing your will, and continually
drawing you to Himself, you can do nothing. (Elias
Boudinot, president of Continental Congress; framer of
the Bill of Rights)[14]

Being a Christian is a character which I prize far above
all this world has or can boast. (Patrick Henry, American
Revolution leader; only governor of Virginia ever to be
elected five times)[15]

The Bible is the best of all books, for it is the Word of
God and teaches us the way to be happy in this world and
in the next. Continue therefore to read it and to regulate
your life by its precepts. (John Jay, original chief justice
of the United States Supreme Court)[16]

I rely upon the merits of Jesus Christ for a pardon of
all my sins. (Samuel Adams, signer of the Declaration
of Independence; father of the American Revolution;
governor of Massachusetts)[17]

No man, whatever be his character or whatever be his
hope, shall enter into rest unless he be reconciled to God
through Jesus Christ. (John Witherspoon, signer of the
Declaration of Independence)[18]

Although John Witherspoon was not a delegate to the Constitutional
Convention, this Scottish minister and lawyer, from his position as president and professor of law at Princeton College, is historically acknowledged

as the one who was most influential in our Constitution's composition. Witherspoon taught law and biblical principles to a number of the delegates who participated in the writing of the Constitution, including a young James Madison, who would soon become the most prominent framer of the Constitution and the primary author and champion of the Bill of Rights.

As should be obvious by now, the atheists, secularists, liberals, and Gnostics are not content to simply leave those who believe in Jesus Christ alone. For whatever reason, they feel compelled to undermine, distort, and destroy "the faith which was once for all delivered to the saints."[19] The founders of our Constitution saw fit to make sure that the citizens of America were guaranteed religious freedom. However, if we sit back and let the skeptics continue to dominate our government, our courts, our media, and our educational system, those guarantees will be lost.

A Planet Divided

Whoever heard of anyone smashing their thumb with a hammer and yelling out the name of Aristotle, or Kierkegaard, or Nietzsche? When we watch today's movies, why aren't the names of Buddha, or Muhammad, or the Reverend Moon cursed by our favorite actors? Why is it always Jesus or God? It's interesting to note that even within the realm of cursing, Jesus remains unique.

I find it amazing that Hollywood, which proclaims that money is its bottom line, continues to alienate what is arguably its largest potential audience by filling nearly all of the films it produces with blasphemies and moral aberrations. Jonathan Falwell, son of the late evangelist, sent me an e-mail in which he lamented over a number of Hollywood productions that in the past few years have overtly ridiculed the Lord—including *Hamlet 2*, a movie that features the song "Rock Me, Sexy Jesus."

> It's this "who cares" attitude regarding depictions of Jesus that leads me to fear that our nation has lost any clear notion of who Jesus is. And as a result of this growing national ignorance, we are witnessing this mounting wave of antagonism and ridicule regarding our Savior.[20]

Why would the media with its ability to reach untold millions refuse to present the reality about the countless lives that have been transformed for the better by Jesus Christ? Why would the promoters of Gnosticism argue against the mountains of irrefutable evidence that prove that the Scriptures contained within the pages of the Bible are accurate? Why would the religious leaders at the time of Jesus do everything in their power to keep the truth about Him from getting out? And why would so many throughout history try to keep others from knowing how easy it is to receive eternal life? The answer lies in the fact that we are in the midst of a spiritual battle—a battle for the will.

The religious leaders during that first century saw with their own eyes the miracles, the healings, the wisdom, the resurrection, and the fulfillment of ancient prophecies. Yet they did not believe. Why did they reject Him? They couldn't use evidence, or logic, or the Scriptures, or some moral flaw of Jesus to support their decision. The only thing that stood in their way of accepting the claims of Christ was their *will*. The same holds true today.

As time forges ahead, the chasm between the supporters and the critics of Jesus Christ will continue to widen. As the prophesied events of the *last days* unfold before us, people will no longer be able to ignore the Man from Nazareth and remain on the fence. Although there are some who think they would prefer to stay neutral if they could and just go about their daily lives on their own accord, that is not really an option in this life—especially once you realize we are in the midst of a battle. If life is a preparation for eternity, and there are only two options available as to where that eternity will be spent, then a decision must be made at some point. To avoid a decision about Christ is to decide against Him.

Forsaken by God

On the day of the crucifixion, there was a period between noon and 3 p.m. when the sky became dark. It was at this time that Jesus cried out from the cross …

> Now from the sixth hour until the ninth hour there was darkness over all the land. And about the ninth hour Jesus cried out with a loud voice, saying, "Eli, Eli, lama sabach-thani?" that is, "My God, My God, why have You forsaken Me?" (Matthew 27:45–46)

Some scholars have suggested that it was during this three-hour period that the sins of the world—past, present, and future—were placed upon Jesus. Every sin that had ever been committed by anyone up until that point, plus every sin that would ever be committed by anyone in the future, even by people yet to be born, was placed on Him. And He paid for them all with His perfect life. What this means is that everyone who has lived, is living, or will ever live on this planet has a fully paid pardon with his or her name on it. And that pardon is freely offered to all who will accept it. But like any earthly pardon, it won't go into effect and become valid until it is accepted.

But why did Jesus think that the Father had forsaken Him while on the cross? It was because He was feeling the effects of sin for the first time in His existence. Jesus was sinless and thus had never lost fellowship with His Holy Father. But in order to become the sacrifice for our sins, He had to take upon Himself the sins of all others.

> For He made Him who knew no sin to be sin for us,
> that we might become the righteousness of God in Him.
> (2 Corinthians 5:21)

A Matter of Choice

Many faced with the prospect of choosing between heaven and hell have wondered how a loving God could ever send anyone to hell. Actually, God is not the one who decides. Those who end up in hell go there by their own choice. Let me explain ...

Contrary to the atheistic belief that it all ends at the moment of death, the Bible makes it clear that *everyone* will be resurrected after dying. But where will everyone go? For those who have accepted Jesus' pardon for their sins, there is heaven. These people will be able to enjoy being in their Creator's presence for all eternity because their sins have been erased—*it will be as if they never sinned.*

Simply trying hard to be good in order to get into heaven doesn't work. We all need to have our sins erased, no matter how great or how small, because there will be no sin in heaven. Just think—no crime, no murder, no lies, no pain, and no tears.[21]

However, those who die without accepting this free pardon will stand before Christ at the final judgment *with their sins still intact!* Remember, when Adam and Eve sinned, they immediately tried to hide from God … similar to when we were bad as children, we instinctively tried to hide from our parents. And just like Adam and Eve in the garden, these people will not be able to endure being in His presence for two seconds, let alone an eternity in heaven. As a result, they will choose to spend their eternity alone, separated from God.

Putting It All Together

> Simon Peter answered Him, "Lord, to whom shall we go? You have the words of eternal life. Also we have come to believe and know that You are the Christ, the Son of the living God." (John 6:68–69)

Most people instinctively know, or at least hope, that there is more to life than just this present life. Jesus, as the Son of God, is the only person ever to have lived who is truly qualified to offer eternal life to the world. No one in their right mind would pass up an offer to share in the blessings of heaven.

Atheists have used their God-given intelligence to come up with reasons and excuses not to believe in God. Yet ultimately, they have nothing else to offer. Islam offers a perverted vision of heaven that appeals primarily to self-absorbed men. The Hindu religion states that all paths, no matter how contradictory, lead to God. To those followers of Hinduism I always suggest they choose Jesus, since they claim all paths are apparently valid anyway.

The Judeo-Christian creator God, through Jesus Christ, offers peace and happiness beyond comprehension forevermore to both men and women—eternal life in heaven—which is the desire of every human heart.

> For God so loved the world that He gave His only begot-
> ten Son, that whoever believes in Him should not perish
> but have everlasting life. (John 3:16)

Noted writer C. S. Lewis, author of the Chronicles of Narnia series and esteemed Oxford faculty member, changed from being an agnostic bordering on atheism to an ardent believer in Jesus at the age of thirty after studying the life of Christ. He concluded there were only three positions a person could come to about Jesus: He was either *a liar* (but liars don't provide the world's greatest wisdom or present an example of holy living); *a madman* (but madmen don't espouse the loftiest teachings ever to be immortalized in writing); or … *the Son of God* (which is exactly what He claimed to be).[22] Which description do you think makes the most sense?

The fascination with Jesus has been going strong now for two thousand years and shows no sign of slowing down. With each passing day there will continue to be those who love Him and those who hate Him. There will be those who wish to know the truth and those who wish to distort it. And there will be those who choose to accept His free gift of eternal life and those who choose to reject it.

The battle continues …

Epilogue

By now you should be able to see why the world has been fascinated by Jesus Christ for two thousand years. The question is, can you believe in a Savior like that? Have you put your eternal destiny in His hands by calling on Him to forgive your sins and save your soul? Jesus said, "Most assuredly, I say to you, he who believes in me has everlasting life." (John 6:47). The decision is yours to make. Remember, it is a decision that will last forever. If you've never done so, I urge you to consider praying the following prayer today …

> Dear God, I believe Jesus Christ is Your Son who died for my sins and for those of the whole world. I believe He was buried and rose from the dead on the third day. Today, I confess that I am a sinner and invite You into my life to cleanse me and save me as You promised. I surrender my life into Your keeping. Amen.

Notes

Chapter 1 Why Jesus?

1   B. A. Robinson "Religions on the World: Number of Adherents; Growth Rates," Ontario Consultants on Religious Tolerance, http://www.religioustolerance.org/worldrel.htm (accessed March 18, 2009).

2   *Encyclopaedia Britannica,* 2007 ed., s.v. "Plato."

3   Acts 6:8—7:60.

4   H. G. Wells, *The Outline of History* (Garden City, NY: Garden City Publishing Co., 1920), 493–534.

5   *Encyclopaedia Britannica,* 2007 ed., s.v. "Bill Clinton."

6   Mark Twain, *The Innocents Abroad* (New York: Signet Classics, 1980), 385.

7   "The Innocents Abroad," Wikipedia, http://en.wikipedia.org/wiki/The_Innocents_Abroad (accessed March 18, 2009).

8   Time Archive, *Time,* http://www.time.com/time/coversearch.

9   Ibid.

10 David Mehegan, "Thriller Instinct," *Boston Globe,* May 8, 2004.

11 "Movies: The Da Vinci Code," Box Office Mojo, http://www.boxofficemojo.com/movies/?id=davincicode.htm.

12 "Movies: The Passion of the Christ," Box Office Mojo, http://www.boxofficemojo.com/movies/?id=passionofthechrist.htm.

Chapter 2 Jesus and His Best-Selling Book

1   Russell Ash, *The Top 10 of Everything, 1997* (New York: DK, 1996), 112.

2   Daniel Radosh, "The Good Book Business: Why Publishers Love the Bible," *New Yorker*, December 18, 2006.

3   Josephus *Contra Apionem* 1:42.

4   "Dead Sea Scrolls," Wikipedia, http://en.wikipedia.org/wiki/Dead_Sea_Scrolls (accessed March 18, 2009).

5   Randall Price, *Searching for the Original Bible* (Eugene, OR: Harvest House, 2007), 57.

6   Ibid., 62–65.

7   Gleason Archer Jr., *A Survey of Old Testament Introduction* (Chicago: Moody, 1974), 25.

8   Norman Geisler, *False Gods of Our Time* (Eugene, OR: Harvest House, 1985), 129.

9   Frederick F. Bruce, *The New Testament Documents: Are They Reliable?* (Downers Grove, IL: InterVarsity Press, 1960), 15.

10 Clark Pinnock, quoted in Josh McDowell, *Skeptics Who Demanded a Verdict* (Wheaton, IL: Tyndale House, 1989), 84.

11 Price, *The Original Bible,* 143–144.

12 Ibid., 154.

13 "Higher Criticism," Wikipedia, http://en.wikipedia.org/wiki/Higher_criticism (accessed March 18, 2009).

14 "David Strauss," Wikipedia, http://en.wikipedia.org/wiki/David_Friedrich_Strauss (accessed March 18, 2009).

15 William Ramsay, *St. Paul the Traveler and the Roman Citizen* (Grand Rapids, MI: Baker, 1949), 8.

16 Geisler, *False Gods of Our Time*, 134–135.

17 Millar F. Burrows, *What Mean These Stones?* (New Haven, CT: American Schools of Oriental Research, 1941), 1.

18 Randall Price, *The Stones Cry Out* (Eugene, OR: Harvest House, 1997), 25.

19 Nelson Glueck, *Rivers in the Desert* (New York: Farrar, Strauss, & Cudahy, 1959), 136.

20 Price, *The Original Bible*, 28.

21 Daniel B. Wallace, "The Gospel according to Bart," Biblical Studies Foundation, http://www.bible.org/page.php?page_id=4000.

22 Neely Tucker, "The Book of Bart: In the Bestseller *Misquoting Jesus*, Agnostic Author Bart Ehrman Picks Apart the Gospels That Made a Disbeliever Out of Him," *Washington Post*, March 5, 2006.

23 Sara James, "The Mystery of the Jesus Papers," *Dateline NBC,* April 2, 2006. Also Lester Holt, *The Today Show*, NBC, March 28, 2006.

24 Associated Press, "Excerpts from the Da Vinci Code Lawsuit," *USA Today,* April 7, 2006.

25 James, "The Mystery of the Jesus Papers."

26 For two such examples see Craig A. Evans, *Fabricating Jesus* (Downers Grove, IL: InterVarsity Press, 2006), 208–217. Also Wallace, "The Gospel according to Bart."

27 Price, *The Original Bible*, 14.

28 Evans, *Fabricating Jesus,* 204.

29 Price, *The Original Bible*, 29.

30 G. K. Chesterton, "The Oracle of the Dog," *Nash's Magazine,* December 1923.

Chapter 3 All Signs Point His Way

1   "Blavatsky Net: Theosophy," Blavatsky New Foundation, http://www.blavatsky.net.

2   "Nostradamus," Nostradamus.org, http://www.nostradamus.org/bio.php

3   "When was Daniel Written?," Spiritual Technology, http://www. harvardhouse.com/Daniel_date-written.htm (accessed April 13, 2009).

4   Theodor H. Gaster, *The Dead Sea Scriptures* (Garden City, NY: Doubleday, 1956).

5   R. K. Harrison, *Biblical Criticism: Historical, Literary, and Textual* (Grand Rapids, MI: Zondervan, 1978).

6   Michael D. Lemonick, "Are the Bible's Stories True?" *Time*, December 18, 1995, 67.

7   Ibid.

8   Alfred Edersheim, The Life and Times of Jesus the Messiah, (New York: Randolph, 1883), quoted in Tim LaHaye, *Why Believe in Jesus?* (Eugene: Harvest House, 2004), 178.

9   Matthew 24:29–31; Mark 13:24–27; Luke 21:25–28; Revelation 19:11–21.

10 Luke 24:13–32.

11 Peter Stoner, *Science Speaks: Scientific Proof of the Accuracy of Prophecy and the Bible* (Chicago: Moody Press, 1963), 109–110.

Chapter 4 Who Else Can Do These Things?

1   See also Mark 6:30–44; Luke 9:10–17; John 6:1–14.

2   Matthew 15:32–38; Mark 8:1–9.

3   Isaiah 14:12–15; Revelation 12:7–9.

4   For a fully documented recent example see Richard E. Gallagher, "A Case of Demonic Possession," *New Oxford Review* 75, no.2 (March 2008).

5   Dave Hunt, *The Occult Invasion* (Eugene, OR: Harvest House, 1998). See Entire chapter 10: "Drugs, Imagination and the Occult." See also David Stern *The Jewish New Testament Commentary* (Clarksville: Messianic Jewish Resources International, 1992), Revelation 9:21.

6   There are no examples of the restoration of sight in the Old Testament. This ability is a unique attribute of the Messiah. See Isaiah 29:18, 35:5, 42:7, 42:16. Also Luke 4:18.

7   Oliver Sacks, *An Anthropologist on Mars* (New York: Alfred A. Knopf, 1995), 108–152. See also *At First Sight* directed by Irwin Winkler, (Hollywood, CA: MGM, 1999).

8   Russell Grigg, "Walking Trees: Modern Science Helps Us Understand a Puzzling Miracle," *Creation* 21 no. 4, (September 1999): 54–55.

9   "David Hume," Wikipedia, http://en.wikipedia.org/wiki/David_Hume (accessed March 18, 2009).

10   Steven Waldman, "Separating 'Diamonds' from 'the Dunghill': The Fascinating History of the 'Jefferson Bible,'" Beliefnet, http://www.beliefnet.com/story/230/story_23039_1.html.

11   Peter Jennings, "The Search for Jesus," *ABC News*, June 26, 2000, is one such example.

12   "The Jesus Seminar," Westar Institute, http://www.westarinstitute.org/Seminars/seminars.html (accessed April 13, 2009).

13   Robert W. Funk and Roy W. Hoover, *The Five Gospels: The Search for the Authentic Words of Jesus* (New York: Macmillan, 1993).

14   Robert W. Funk, *The Acts of Jesus: The Search for the Authentic Deeds of Jesus* (San Francisco: HarperSanFrancisco, 1998).

Chapter 5 The Greatest Prophet

1   Grant R. Jeffrey, *Heaven: The Last Frontier* (Toronto: Frontier Research Publications, 1990), 76.

2   Ibid., 76–79.

3   Matthew 3:1–12; Mark 1:2–8; Luke 3:1–20; John 1:19–28.

4   See also Matthew 3:13–17; Mark 1:9–11; Luke 3:21–22.

5   Josephus *War of the Jews,* vol. 7, 1.1.

6   Josephus *War of the Jews,* vol. 6, 9.3.

7   Eusebius *Church History,* vol. 3, 5:3.

8   "Religions of the World," http://www.religioustolerance.org/worldrel. htm.

9   Revelation 13:16–18.

10 Revelation 14:9–11.

11 Revelation 20:4.

12 Revelation 6:8; Revelation 9:15–18; Revelation 20:4; millions of additional deaths will occur as a result of the remaining judgments totaling approximately three-fourths of the world's population.

13 Matthew 24; Mark 13; Luke 21.

14 See Matthew 24:34; Mark 13:30.

Chapter 6 Everybody Knows He Rose

1   Wilbur M. Smith, *Therefore, Stand* (Boston: W. A. Wilde Co., 1945), 346–347.

2   Hugh J. Schonfield, *The Passover Plot* (New York: Bantam Books, 1967).

3   See also *The Passover Plot,* directed by Michael Campus, Atlas Film Corporation, 1976.

4   Schonfield, *The Passover Plot*, 163.

5   Michael Baigent, *The Jesus Papers: Exposing the Greatest Cover-up in History* (San Francisco: HarperSanFrancisco, 2006), 128–129.

6   Ibid., 123.

7   James D. Tabor, *The Jesus Dynasty* (New York: Simon & Schuster, 2006), 235.

8   Ibid., 228.

9   Josh McDowell, "Evidence for the Resurrection," Josh McDowell Ministry, 1992, http://www.leaderu.com/everystudent/easter/articles/josh2.html.

10 E. M. Blaiklock, quoted in Josh McDowell, *Skeptics Who Demanded*, 85.

11 Paul Althaus, *Die Wahrheit des Kirchlichen Osterglaubens* (Gutersloh, Germany: C. Bertelsmann, 1941), 22.

12 Edwin M. Yamauchi, quoted in McDowell, "Evidence for the Resurrection."

13 Thomas Arnold, quoted in McDowell, "Evidence for the Resurrection."

14 Wilbur M. Smith, *The Supernaturalness of Christ* (Boston: W. A. Wilde Co., 1940), 206–207.

15 David Strauss, *The Life of Jesus, for the People* (London: Williams and Norgate, 1879), 412.

16 Jennings, "The Search for Jesus."

17 Simon Greenleaf, *The Testimony of the Evangelists: Examined by the Rules of Evidence Administered in Courts of Justice* (Grand Rapids, MI: Baker, 1965), 29.

Chapter 7 Look How He Loves

1 Tanya Eiserer, Scott Farwell, and Scott Goldstein, "Lewisville Cab Driver Had Been Investigated for Previous Abuse," *Dallas Morning News,* January 9, 2008.

2 Wendy Hundley, "Lewisville Cabdriver Sought in Slayings of 2 Teen Daughters," *Dallas Morning News,* January 2, 2008.

3 Eiserer, Farwell, and Goldstein, "Lewisville Cab Driver Had Been Investigated."

4 Tanya Eiserer, "Slain Lewisville Sisters Mourned at Christian, Muslim Services," *Dallas Morning News,* January 6, 2008.

5 Eiserer, Farwell, and Goldstein, "Lewisville Cab Driver Had Been Investigated."

6 Ibid.

7 Ibid.

8 John Walsh, *America's Most Wanted*, Fox Television, January 5, 2008.

9   Bud Gillett, "Family of Slain Sisters Wants Father to Come Forth," *CBS News,* January 5, 2008.

10 Eiserer, Farwell, and Goldstein, "Lewisville Cab Driver Had Been Investigated."

11 Cinnamon Stillwell, "Honor Killings: When the Ancient and the Modern Collide," *San Francisco Chronicle,* January 23, 2008.

12 Hillary Mayell, "Thousands of Women Killed for Family 'Honor,'" *National Geographic News*, February 12, 2002.

13 Stillwell, "Honor Killings."

14 Surah 2:282.

15 Hassan M. Fattah, "Saudi Arabia Debates Women's Right to Drive," *New York Times,* September 28, 2007.

16 Surah 4:11.

17 Lisa Beyer, "The Women of Islam," *Time*, November 25, 2001.

18 Joseph Farah, "IslamicTerror.com?," *WorldNetDaily,* November 13, 2001, http://www.worldnetdaily.com/index.php?fa=PAGE.view&pageId=11651

19 Cal Thomas, "Surrender!" *Salem Web Network,* July 8, 2008, http://townhall.com/columnists/CalThomas/2008/07/08/Surrender!

20 Ibid.

21 Charles Albert Savage, *The Athenian Family: A Sociological and Legal Study* (Baltimore: Johns Hopkins Press, 1907), 29.

22 H. D. F. Kitto, *The Greeks* (Chicago: Aldine Publishing, 1964), 231.

23 Aristotle *Politics*, vol. 1, 1260, quoted in Alvin J. Schmidt, *How Christianity Changed the World* (Grand Rapids: Zondervan, 2004), 99.

24 John Boswell, *The Kindness of Strangers* (New York: Pantheon Books, 1988), 4.

25 John P. Balsdon, *Roman Women: Their History and Habits* (New York: John Day, 1963), 276.

26 Rudolph Sohm, *The Institutes of Roman Law*, trans. James C. Ledlie (Oxford: Clarendon Press, 1892), 365.

27 Ibid., 389.

28 L. F. Cervantes, *New Catholic Encyclopedia*, vol. 14 (New York: McGraw-Hill, 1967), s.v. "Woman."

29 Talmud, Sotah 3.4.

30 Schmidt, *How Christianity Changed the World*, 108.

31 Ibid., 107.

32 Genesis 1:27.

33 William C. Morey, *Outlines of Roman Law* (New York: Putnam & Sons, 1894), 150.

34 Genesis 2:21–24.

35 See the Mormon publication Doctrine and Covenants, Section 132; given to Joseph Smith by "divine revelation" in Nauvoo, Illinois, July 12, 1843.

36 James Brooke, "Utah Struggles with Revival of Polygamy," *New York Times*, August 23, 1998.

37 Ibn Warraq, "Virgins? What Virgins?" *The Guardian*, January 12, 2002.

Chapter 8 They Still Don't Know What They Are Doing

1 "Nag Hammadi Library," Wikipedia, http://en.wikipedia.org/wiki/Nag_Hammadi_library (accessed March 18, 2009).

2 "Elaine Pagels," Wikipedia, http://en.wikipedia.org/wiki/Elaine_Pagels (accessed March 18, 2009).

3 Mark C. Henrie, ed., "The Fifty Worst (and Best) Books of the Century," *The Intercollegiate Review* 35, no.1 (Fall 1999): 6.

4 Damian Thompson, "How Da Vinci Code Tapped Pseudo-Fact Hunger," *Telegraph*, January 13, 2008.

5 Dan Brown, *The Da Vinci Code* (New York: Doubleday, 2003), 253–254.

6   Jennings, "The Search for Jesus."

7   Ibid.

8   Mehegan, "Thriller Instinct."

9   "Elaine Pagels," Wikipedia.

10 Mehegan, "Thriller Instinct."

11 James, "The Mystery of The Jesus Papers."

12 "Movies: The Da Vinci Code," Box Office Mojo.

13 "The Da Vinci Code," Sony Pictures, http://sonypictures.com/
    homevideo/thedavincicode/index.html.

14 Helmut Koester, *Ancient Christian Gospels: Their History and
    Development* (Philadelphia: Trinity Press International, 1990), 84–85.

15 Craig A. Evans, "Refuting the New Controversial Theories About
    Jesus," program #3, *The John Ankerberg Show:* (Chattanooga: Ankerberg
    Theological Research Institute, 2006).

16 For a plausible account of the conflict between the aged apostle John
    and the Gnostic promoter Cerinthus who built a school of Gnosticism
    in Ephesus that ultimately failed, see the author's book cowritten with
    Jerry B. Jenkins titled *John's Story: The Last Eyewitness* (New York:
    Penguin Group, 2006), chapters 3 and 4.

17 Brown, *The Da Vinci Code,* 231.

18 Elaine Pagels, *Beyond Belief: The Secret Gospel of Thomas* (New York:
    Random House, 2003), 75.

19 John 20:3–8.

20 Kurt Rudolph, *Gnosis: The Nature and History of Gnosticism* (Edinburgh:
    T&T Clark, 1983), 57-59.

21 "Gospel of Thomas," Wikipedia, http://en.wikipedia.org/wiki/Gospel_
    of_Thomas (accessed April 13, 2009).

22 Craig A. Evans, *Fabricating Jesus* (Downers Grove, IL: InterVarsity
    Press, 2006), 71–77.

23 Stephen J. Patterson, James M. Robinson, and Hans-Gebhard Bethge,
    The Fifth Gospel (Harrisburg: Trinity Press International, 1998).

24 Ibid.

25 Ibid.

26 Ibid.

27 Ibid.

28 Darrell L. Bock, "What About the Missing Gospels?" program #2, *The John Ankerberg Show:* (Chattanooga: Ankerberg Theological Research Institute, 2006).

29 M. P. Nilsson, *Opuscula Selecta: Linguis Anglica, Francogallica, Germanica Conscripta,* vol. 3 (Lund: CWK Gleerup, 1960), 346.

30 Elaine Pagels, *The Gnostic Gospels* (New York: Random House, 1979), xxxi.

31 Walter Bauer, *Orthodoxy and Heresy in Earliest Christianity* (London: SCM Press, 1964), xxi.

32 Helmut Koester, "The Origin and Nature of Diversification in the History of Early Christianity," *Harvard Theological Review,* (1965): 114.

33 Hans-Dietrich Altendorf, "Zum Stichwort: Rechtglabigkeit und Ketzerei im altesten Christentum," *Zeitschrift für Kirchengeschichte,* 1969, 64.

34 Simone Pétrement, *A Separate God: The Origins and Teachings of Gnosticism* (San Francisco: HarperSanFrancisco, 1984), quoted in Bock, *The Missing Gospels,* (Nashville: Thomas Nelson, 2006). 28.

35 James M. Robinson, ed., "The Gospel of Philip" #134, in *The Nag Hammadi Library* (San Francisco: HarperCollins, 1990).

36 Ibid., #105.

37 James M. Robinson, ed., "The Apocryphon of John" in *The Nag Hammadi Library* (San Francisco: HarperCollins, 1990), #5.

38 Ibid., #10.

39 Ibid., #18.

40 James M. Robinson, ed., "The Apocalypse of Peter" in *The Coptic Gnostic Library: A Complete Edition of the Nag Hammadi Codices* (Leiden, Netherlands: Brill, 2000), 4:241–243.

41 Robinson, "The Apocryphon of John," #3.

42 James M. Robinson, ed., "The Sophia of Jesus Christ" in *The Nag Hammadi Library* (San Francisco: HarperCollins, 1990).

43 Baigent, *The Jesus Papers*, 88.

44 Associated Press, "Basic Instinct Director Paul Verhoeven: Jesus Was Son of Mary and Roman Rapist," *Fox News*, April 23, 2008.

45 Robinson, "The Apocryphon of John," #20.

46 Price, *The Original Bible*, 183–185.

47 Irenaeus *Against Heresies*, vol. 1, 31-1.

48 Bart D. Ehrman, *The Lost Gospel of Judas Iscariot: A New Look at Betrayer and Betrayed* (Oxford: University Press, 2006), 180.

49 Pagels, *Beyond Belief*, quoted in Baigent, *The Jesus Papers*, 84.

Chapter 9 Now As Always, Jesus Changes Lives

1   Romans 1:16.

2   Robert S. Hogg, et al., "Modelling the Impact of HIV Disease on Mortality in Gay and Bisexual Men," *International Journal of Epidemiology* 26, no.3, (1997): 657.

3   Paul L. Tan, *Encyclopedia of 7700 Illustrations* (Garland: Bible Communications, 1979), 174, quoted in D. James Kennedy and Jerry Newcombe, *What If Jesus Had Never Been Born?* (Nashville: Thomas Nelson, 1994), 189.

4   Jeb Stuart Magruder, *An American Life: One Man's Road to Watergate* (New York: Atheneum, 1974), 69.

5   Kennedy, *What If Jesus Had Never Been Born?*, 199.

Chapter 10 Who Do You Say I Am?

1   David Brickner, *Future Hope* (Chicago: Moody Publishers, 2002), 73.

2   "Battle of Megiddo," Wikipedia, http://en.wikipedia.org/wiki/Battle_
    of_Megiddo_%2815th_century_BC%29 (accessed March 18, 2009).

3   Revelation 16:16.

4   Matthew 24:21–30; Mark 13:19–26; Luke 21:25–28.

5   Revelation 20:4.

6   Walter H. Bidwell, *The Eclectic Magazine of Foreign Literature, Science,
    and Art,* vol. 7 (New York: Leavitt, Trow & Co., 1868), 770.

7   "Religious Affiliation of the Founding Fathers of the United States of
    America," Adherents.com, http://www.adherents.com/gov/Founding_
    Fathers_Religion.html (accessed March 18, 2009).

8   Jennifer Tomase, "The Tale of John Harvard's Surviving Book,"
    Harvard University Gazette Online, November 1, 2007, http://www.
    news.harvard.edu/gazette/2007/11.01/13-johnharvard.html.

9   Associated Press, "Harvard to Investigate Origins of Life," *Washington
    Times,* August 15, 2005.

10 John Adams, *The Works of John Adams, Second President of the United
    States,* vol. 3, ed. Charles F. Adams (Boston: Little, Brown, and Co.,
    1856), 421. Diary entry for July 26, 1796.

11 John Quincy Adams, *An Oration Delivered Before the Inhabitants of
    the Town of Newburyport at Their Request on the 61st Anniversary of
    the Declaration of Independence, July 4, 1837* (Newburyport: Charles
    Whipple, 1837), 5–6.

12 Benjamin Rush, *Letters of Benjamin Rush,* vol. 1, ed. L. H. Butterfield
    (Princeton: American Philosophical Society, 1951), 475. Statement
    made July 9, 1788.

13 John Hancock, *A Proclamation for a Day of Public Thanksgiving 1791,*
    given as governor of the Commonwealth of Massachusetts.

14 Elias Boudinot, *The Age of Revelation* (Philadelphia: Asbury Dickens,
    1801) xii–xiv. Statement made on October 30, 1782.

15 Samuel Greene Arnold, *The Life of Patrick Henry of Virginia* (Auburn
    and Buffalo: Miller, Orton, and Mulligan, 1854), 249–250.

16 John Jay, *John Jay: The Winning of the Peace—Unpublished Papers 1780-1784,* vol. 2, ed. Richard B. Morris (New York: Harper & Row Publishers, 1980), 709. Statement made April 8, 1784.

17 Samuel Adams, *Life and Public Services of Samuel Adams,* vol. 3, ed. William V. Wells (Boston: Little, Brown, and Co., 1865), 379. From the last will and testament of Samuel Adams.

18 John Witherspoon, *The Works of John Witherspoon*, vol. 5, (Edinburgh: J. Ogle, 1815), 245. Statement made January 2, 1758.

19 Jude 1:3.

20 Jonathan Falwell, e-mail message to author, July 25, 2008.

21 Revelation 21:3–4.

22 C. S. Lewis, *Mere Christianity* (New York: MacMillan Publishing Co., 1960), 40–41.

About the Authors

Rick Parker, Parker Photography

Author, speaker, and minister Dr. Tim LaHaye has written or coauthored more than sixty books, including the New York Times best-selling Left Behind series. A pastor for thirty-nine years, there's nothing Dr. LaHaye likes to talk about more than Jesus. Dr. LaHaye and his wife, Beverly, reside in Southern California. You can learn more about Dr. LaHaye and his work at TimLaHaye.com.

David Minasian is a motion-picture writer, producer, and director with twenty-five years of experience in the film industry. Since 2002, he has worked closely with Tim LaHaye as a cowriter and researcher. David lives with his wife, Erin, and their children in Southern California.

Shannon Bolline